PRENTICE HALL
WORLD STUDIES

Test Prep Workbook

Boston, Massachusetts
Upper Saddle River, New Jersey

Copyright © by Pearson Education, Inc., publishing as Pearson Prentice Hall, Boston, Massachusetts 02116.
All rights reserved. Printed in the United States of America. This publication is protected by copyright, and permission should be obtained from the publisher prior to any prohibited reproduction, storage in a retrieval system or transmission in any form or by any means, electronic, mechanical, photocopying, recording, or likewise. For information regarding permission(s), write to: Rights and Permissions Department.

ISBN 0-13-128420-7

6 7 8 9 10   08 07 06

Table of Contents

How To Use This Book v

Practice Tests

Africa Practice Tests A, B, and C 1

The Ancient World Practice Tests A, B, and C 13

Asia and the Pacific Practice Tests A, B, and C 25

Europe and Russia Practice Tests A, B, and C 37

Foundations of Geography Practice Tests A, B, and C 49

Latin America Practice Tests A, B, and C 61

Medieval Times to Today Practice Tests A, B, and C 73

The United States and Canada Practice Tests A, B, and C 85

Study Sheets

Africa Study Sheet 97

The Ancient World Study Sheet 100

Asia and the Pacific Study Sheet 103

Europe and Russia Study Sheet 110

Foundations of Geography Study Sheet 113

Latin America Study Sheet 116

Medieval Times to Today Study Sheet 120

The United States and Canada Study Sheet 124

© Pearson Education, Inc., publishing as Pearson Prentice Hall. All rights reserved.

How To Use This Book

The *World Studies Test Prep Workbook* contains multiple-choice test questions written specifically for Prentice Hall's *World Studies* program. This booklet will help you prepare for World Studies tests in the followings ways:

The test questions provide practice in answering multiple-choice questions.

Even when you have studied for a test, you may sometimes choose an incorrect answer because you have not processed the test question correctly. For example, you may make a mistake because you have not read the stem or the answer choices carefully. The questions in this booklet will give you practice in successfully processing and answering multiple-choice questions.

The test questions help you prepare for standardized and end-of-course exams.

Standardized and end-of-course exams often are long tests containing many test questions. They usually include multiple-choice questions. Some tests consist of no other type of test item! Taking practice tests that mirror the quantity and type of test items on standardized assessments may help you when you take the actual test.

Your teacher will tell you when and how to take the tests in this booklet. You can practice taking a test in the same amount of time you will have in the real test-taking setting.

The test questions help you make sure you have suitably studied the material.

Test preparation includes much more than taking practice tests. You must have read and studied the course material properly so that you can recall and apply the facts and concepts you've learned. Taking practice tests is not the same as studying effectively. However, taking a practice test will help you measure how well you have studied the subject. If you are disappointed in your results, use the Study Sheets at the back of the booklet to supplement your studying.

Name _____ Date _____ Class _____

Africa Practice Test A

Directions: *Read each question and choose the best answer. Then write the letter for the answer you have chosen in each blank.*

_____ 1. What is the word that describes the raised, level areas of land that cover much of the African continent?
- **A.** mountain
- **B.** plateau
- **C.** lake
- **D.** desert

_____ 2. Most of Africa is located between the
- **A.** Equator and the Tropic of Cancer.
- **B.** Indian Ocean and the Pacific Ocean.
- **C.** Tropic of Cancer and the Tropic of Capricorn.
- **D.** Namib Desert and the Kalahari Desert.

_____ 3. Lions, elephants, and zebras live in the most common type of vegetation region found in Africa. This vegetation region is known as the
- **A.** rainforest.
- **B.** savanna.
- **C.** desert.
- **D.** coastal plain.

_____ 4. What are typical cash crops grown in Africa?
- **A.** pineapples, tea, and cacao beans
- **B.** yams, corn, and pineapples
- **C.** coffee, cacao beans, and tea
- **D.** potatoes, tomatoes, and indigo

_____ 5. What were the Bantu migrations?
- **A.** Movement of people from North Africa to Europe
- **B.** Movement of rainforest from South Africa to North Africa
- **C.** Trade between East Africans and people across the Indian Ocean
- **D.** Movement of people across Africa to Central and Southern Africa

_____ 6. What is a civilization that arose on the Nile River about 5,000 years ago?
- **A.** South Africa
- **B.** Nigeria
- **C.** Egypt
- **D.** Great Zimbabwe

_____ 7. Early East African civilizations grew strong from
- **A.** trade.
- **B.** powerful armies.
- **C.** large farms.
- **D.** mining.

Africa Practice Test A (continued)

_____ 8. Which group of people began to trade with Africa in the 1400s?
   A. Europeans
   B. Asians
   C. Americans
   D. Australians

_____ 9. Before Europeans took over parts of Africa, individual Africans did not buy or sell land because
   A. they were too poor.
   B. in most African countries, the land was owned by the government.
   C. land was granted to a farmer and his family by a ruler.
   D. the very idea of owning land did not exist.

_____ 10. Which is the richest, most urban, and most industrialized country in Africa?
   A. Southern Africa
   B. South Africa
   C. Central Africa
   D. Zambia

_____ 11. Which religions do people in Africa practice?
   A. Islam and Christianity
   B. Buddhism and Islam
   C. Traditional African religions and Judaism
   D. Christianity, Judaism, Islam, and traditional African religions

_____ 12. What is the role of a griot?
   A. to pass on a group's oral traditions to the next generation
   B. to supervise children's education
   C. to advise military leaders
   D. to conduct religious services

_____ 13. The countries that form North Africa are
   A. Kenya, Algeria, Ethiopia, Mali, Egypt.
   B. Egypt, Libya, Tunisia, Algeria, Morocco.
   C. Ethiopia, Nigeria, Mali, Algeria, Egypt.
   D. Niger, Congo, Mali, Nigeria, Algeria.

© Pearson Education, Inc., publishing as Pearson Prentice Hall. All rights reserved.

Name _____ Date _____ Class _____

Africa Practice Test A (continued)

_____ 14. Because most of Algeria is desert, most people live
   A. in desert oases.
   B. on terraces.
   C. in the mountains.
   D. on the coast.

_____ 15. Why was Nigeria's capital moved from Lagos to Abuja?
   A. Lagos represented old British rule to many of Nigeria's people.
   B. Abuja is located in the center of the country and has a more diverse population.
   C. Abuja was the capital of Nigeria before the Europeans arrived.
   D. Many of the new leaders of Nigeria already lived in Abuja.

_____ 16. What important role did Kwame Nkrumah play in the history of Ghana?
   A. He discovered gold along the Gold Coast.
   B. He established the traditional form of government in Ghana.
   C. He established the first British colony on the Gold Coast.
   D. He persuaded the people to demand independence from Great Britain.

_____ 17. Today in the Sahel, people earn their living by
   A. practicing large scale trade.
   B. growing rain forest cash crops.
   C. herding animals and raising crops.
   D. working in factories.

_____ 18. What is one environmental effect of overgrazing by large herds of animals?
   A. overpopulation of the herded animal
   B. price of meat can fall
   C. desertification
   D. soil nourishment

_____ 19. Christians and Muslims in Ethiopia are
   A. always friendly with each other.
   B. always at war with each other.
   C. sometimes friends and sometimes enemies.
   D. rarely in contact.

© Pearson Education, Inc., publishing as Pearson Prentice Hall. All rights reserved.

Africa Practice Test A (continued)

_____ 20. What was the lingua franca that Julius Nyerere established in Tanzania?
- A. Geez
- B. Swahili
- C. French
- D. Arabic

_____ 21. One of the best examples of Kenya's harambee, or pulling together is
- A. Kenyans moving to Nairobi in order to find work.
- B. women's groups forming in order to solve community problems.
- C. various ethnic groups holding on to their traditions.
- D. parents refusing to pay all school costs.

_____ 22. The British wanted to control Afrikaner land after
- A. independence.
- B. Dutch farms failed.
- C. factories were built.
- D. gold and diamonds were discovered there.

_____ 23. What does *apartheid* mean?
- A. to set apart religious groups
- B. to separate government agencies
- C. to break up large businesses
- D. to restrict rights of nonwhites in South Africa

_____ 24. What single ethnic group makes up the majority of South Africa's population?
- A. White
- B. Black
- C. Asian
- D. Xhosa

_____ 25. Who became the first black African president of South Africa?
- A. Nelson Mandela
- B. Kwame Nkrumah
- C. Julius Nyerere
- D. Joseph Mobutu

Name _____ Date _____ Class _____

Africa Practice Test B

Directions: *Read each question and choose the best answer. Then write the letter for the answer you have chosen in each blank.*

_____ 1. Which of these rivers is not located in Africa?
   A. Niger
   B. Congo
   C. Tigris
   D. Nile

_____ 2. Why do Ethiopia and Somalia, two countries that are about the same distance from the Equator, have different climates?
   A. Ethiopia is a desert, and Somalia has many rivers.
   B. Ethiopia has a much higher elevation than Somalia.
   C. Somalia is farther from the Tropic of Cancer than Ethiopia is.
   D. Ethiopia is in western Africa while Somalia is in eastern Africa.

_____ 3. Bantu-speakers moved from their homelands and settled in
   A. North Africa.
   B. West Africa.
   C. East and West Africa.
   D. Central and Southern Africa.

_____ 4. What were some characteristics of ancient Egyptian civilization?
   A. Islam, Swahili language, bronze sculptures
   B. Large pyramids, pharaohs, hieroglyphs
   C. Christianity, gold trade, bronze sculptures
   D. Bantu language, Christianity, homes made of stone

_____ 5. What was the effect of Mansa Musa's pilgrimage to the city of Mecca?
   A. It spread the Islamic faith throughout Europe.
   B. It created new trading ties with other Muslim states, and it displayed Mali's wealth.
   C. It caused hostility throughout Africa, starting wars and limiting trade.
   D. It repaired the broken relationship between Musa and his brother's clan, the Mosas.

_____ 6. How did slavery in the Americas differ from slavery in Africa?
   A. Settlers in America often freed their slaves.
   B. Freed African slaves in America often became important citizens.
   C. European settlers in America rarely freed their slaves.
   D. African slaves in America could buy their fellow slaves.

_____ 7. Where do most people in the North African countries live?
   A. near bodies of water
   B. in the Sahara desert
   C. near mountain ranges
   D. in the Great Rift Valley

© Pearson Education, Inc., publishing as Pearson Prentice Hall. All rights reserved.

Africa Practice Test B (continued)

_____ 8. After achieving independence from European countries, some African nations faced economic problems which often resulted from
   A. a diverse economy that provided jobs in different fields for citizens.
   B. a specialized economy that relied on one product or natural resource.
   C. not joining international organizations.
   D. relying on income taxes.

_____ 9. How is desertification affecting the economy of Mali?
   A. As people leave the cities of Mali, theft has become a problem.
   B. As fertile land becomes too dry, Mali's farmers and herders are threatened.
   C. As the desert areas in Mali become more populated, the economies of the cities suffer.
   D. As the fertile land changes to desert, irrigation companies need more employees.

_____ 10. Why do most Kenyan men who move to the cities for work leave their families behind in rural areas?
   A. It is too hard for the women to find work in the cities, but many jobs are available for men.
   B. It is against the teachings of Islam for women to take jobs in cities.
   C. Families have been targets of ethnic attacks, so they prefer to stay in safety in the country.
   D. Women are the primary caretakers for the children, and it is too expensive to move children to the cities.

_____ 11. What can be the result of relying too much on cash crops?
   A. Less land is planted with crops to feed families, so food shortages result.
   B. Government can become weak because too much power is given to farmers and workers.
   C. Subsistence farmers, angry that cash crop farmers are taking over their land, can create civil unrest.
   D. Cash crop farmers pay higher taxes to the government, which in turn leads to better products and services.

_____ 12. The Aswan High Dam is an engineering marvel that is located in
   A. Ghana.
   B. Tanzania.
   C. Nigeria.
   D. Egypt.

_____ 13. How do most people in rural Egypt make their living?
   A. as factory workers
   B. as farmers
   C. as office workers
   D. as professionals

© Pearson Education, Inc., publishing as Pearson Prentice Hall. All rights reserved.

Africa Practice Test B (continued)

_____ 14. Why is Nigeria considered a culturally diverse country?
   A. There are numerous ethnic groups and more than 200 languages are spoken.
   B. Only two major ethnic groups live in Nigeria.
   C. There are many industrialized cities in Nigeria.
   D. There is only one major religion in the country.

_____ 15. Why did Kwame Nkrumah urge the people of the Gold Coast to seek independence from Great Britain?
   A. He wanted to become independently wealthy.
   B. He desired that France take over the country.
   C. He wanted the people of the country to benefit from the country's natural resources.
   D. He wanted to create an empire.

_____ 16. What was the *ujamaa* program that was established in Tanzania?
   A. a self-help program that rural women established
   B. a program to bring a super highway throughout the country
   C. a program to change the national language
   D. a program of self-reliance for farmers to work together and share resources

_____ 17. People who belonged to the African National Congress (ANC) were
   A. Afrikaners who supported apartheid.
   B. blacks who fought for voting rights.
   C. English who supported apartheid.
   D. blacks and coloreds who did not support equal rights.

_____ 18. What is the main purpose of storytelling for West African cultures?
   A. It's a way of entertaining young children.
   B. It is a way to create stories for new ideas and customs.
   C. It passes down their history and customs to the next generation.
   D. It's a form of entertainment for those who have no television.

_____ 19. A national language can sometime help countries to prevent ethnic conflict by
   A. forcing people to be bilingual.
   B. encouraging people who do not want to speak that language to leave the country.
   C. forbidding people from speaking their native languages and practicing their different customs.
   D. allowing different groups to communicate with one another.

Name _____ Date _____ Class _____

Africa Practice Test B (continued)

_____ 20. After the end of apartheid, South Africans were able to change
- A. immediately to a system that integrated blacks and whites, ending segregation permanently.
- B. the laws that required segregation.
- C. back the laws ending segregation by creating a new, more lenient system of apartheid in 2002.
- D. laws in neighboring countries that also practiced systems of apartheid.

Directions: *Read each question and write your answer on the lines provided.*

21. List three ways in which Africa is diverse.

   _____
   _____
   _____
   _____

22. Describe one African country and its efforts to improve the quality of daily life.

   _____
   _____
   _____
   _____

23. Explain how the ancient city-states in East Africa were able to become wealthy.

   _____
   _____
   _____
   _____

24. Why have many countries in Africa tried to diversify their economies?

   _____
   _____
   _____
   _____

© Pearson Education, Inc., publishing as Pearson Prentice Hall. All rights reserved.

Africa Practice Test C

Directions: *Read each question and choose the best answer. Then write the letter for the answer you have chosen in each blank.*

_____ 1. Mount Kilimanjaro is located near the Equator. How does the elevation of Mount Kilimanjaro affect its climate?

    A. Its elevation does not affect its climate.

    B. The peak of Mount Kilimanjaro is usually hot and humid.

    C. The peak of Mount Kilimanjaro is covered with snow year round.

    D. The elevation of Mount Kilimanjaro is so low that it makes no difference.

_____ 2. Some African countries have been trying to diversify their economies by focusing on

    A. one main cash crop.

    B. traditional farming methods.

    C. subsistence farming.

    D. diversification of crops, raw materials, and manufactured goods.

_____ 3. Why did early city-states in Africa such as Malindi, Mombasa, and Kilwa become powerful?

    A. They were successful at trade, placed taxes on merchants, and controlled surrounding lands.

    B. Their economy was based on agriculture.

    C. They were close to the Nile River and able to travel to various parts of North Africa.

    D. They allowed more powerful nations to run their governments.

_____ 4. North Africa was often invaded by other powers. Which of the following lists these conquering powers in correct chronological order?

    A. Romans, Phoenicians, Chinese

    B. Chinese, Phoenicians, Arabs

    C. Arabs, Phoenicians, Romans

    D. Phoenicians, Romans, Arabs

_____ 5. Other than Islam, what has increasingly influenced North African cultures?

    A. their study of Islamic medicine and health care

    B. new, more advanced farming systems

    C. trade with people in Europe, Asia, and other parts of Africa, which bring in outside influences

    D. the industrialization of large areas of the Sahara

© Pearson Education, Inc., publishing as Pearson Prentice Hall. All rights reserved.

Africa Practice Test C (continued)

_____ 6. How did nationalism affect Africa in the early 1900s?

   A. African countries tried to work with European powers to improve living conditions.
   B. African leaders redrew the boundaries of African countries.
   C. Africans started their own political parties and worked at gaining the right to vote.
   D. European countries willingly gave African countries their independence

_____ 7. What major event in the 1940s, helped African colonies move closer to independence?

   A. the Great Depression
   B. Africa joined the North American Trade Association.
   C. World War II
   D. Ghana won its freedom from Great Britain.

_____ 8. Which of the following is part of the Five Pillars of Islam?

   A. pray five times a day and obey the elders
   B. pray five times a day and give alms to the needy
   C. fast during the night hours of Ramadan
   D. make a pilgrimage to Mecca at least once and obey the elders

_____ 9. How has the Aswan Dam affected life in Egypt?

   A. The dam spreads silt throughout the Nile Delta.
   B. It has prevented irrigation of crops.
   C. Farmers have to use fertilizers which threaten the country's water supply.
   D. It has become a major fishing area in Egypt.

_____ 10. Christianity and Islam spread to Ethiopia because Ethiopia was

   A. not located along trade routes.
   B. looking for a new religion to unify the country.
   C. part of the Roman Empire.
   D. a center of trade and exposed to other cultures and religions.

_____ 11. After African countries gained independence from colonial powers, how were these countries often governed?

   A. All African countries became democracies.
   B. Many African countries were ruled by military governments where people had few rights.
   C. Most African countries were ruled by communists.
   D. Many African countries were ruled by African kings.

© Pearson Education, Inc., publishing as Pearson Prentice Hall. All rights reserved.

Africa Practice Test C (continued)

_____ 12. How did apartheid affect black Africans in South Africa?

    A. They were not allowed the same rights as whites or Europeans.

    B. They were given equal rights to those of the whites and Europeans.

    C. They had economic opportunities to own their own land and businesses.

    D. Even though there was legal segregation between black Africans and whites, the laws were not really enforced.

Directions: *Read each question and write your answer on the lines provided.*

13. How did ancient kingdoms in West Africa develop their power? What kinds of achievements can be noted from these kingdoms?

_____

_____

_____

_____

14. What happened in Ghana following independence?

_____

_____

_____

_____

15. How do East African countries reveal the influence of other cultures?

_____

_____

_____

_____

© Pearson Education, Inc., publishing as Pearson Prentice Hall. All rights reserved.

Africa Practice Test C (continued)

16. In a three-paragraph essay, discuss some of the challenges that African countries faced after winning their independence from imperial powers. What were some of the programs that African leaders proposed once they gained independence?

Name _____ Date _____ Class _____

The Ancient World Practice Test A

Directions: *Read each question and choose the best answer. Then write the letter for the answer you have chosen in each blank.*

_____ 1. Surpluses of food during the New Stone Age encouraged
   A. further migration.
   B. parents to limit the number of their children.
   C. some people to become artisans.
   D. every member of the community to become farmers.

_____ 2. Hammurabi's Code was important because it was
   A. part of the oral tradition.
   B. the first time laws were written down.
   C. the key to learning hieroglyphics.
   D. applied equally to everyone.

_____ 3. Mesopotamia was located
   A. between the Tigris and Euphrates rivers.
   B. in the Indus River Valley.
   C. along the Nile.
   D. along the Ganges.

_____ 4. The Assyrians invented
   A. the battering ram.
   B. the catapult.
   C. cannons.
   D. spears.

_____ 5. In ancient times, scribes were skilled people who could
   A. fight in armies.
   B. design and build.
   C. add and subtract.
   D. read and write.

_____ 6. The Phoenician alphabet was
   A. cuneiform.
   B. the basis of the English alphabet.
   C. very complicated.
   D. not lasting in its influence.

_____ 7. The religion of the Israelites was based on
   A. monotheism, a belief in one god.
   B. polytheism, a belief in many gods.
   C. using no written Bible.
   D. settling in Canaan.

© Pearson Education, Inc., publishing as Pearson Prentice Hall. All rights reserved.

The Ancient World Practice Test A (continued)

_____ 8. Egypt was protected from invasion because of
- A. the flooding of the Nile.
- B. gold from Nubia.
- C. its large navy.
- D. the Sahara desert to the east and west.

_____ 9. Egyptian pharaohs ruled with absolute power over
- A. everyone in Africa.
- B. only priests.
- C. only slaves.
- D. all Egyptians.

_____ 10. How did ancient Egyptians demonstrate their belief in life after death?
- A. They believed in just one god.
- B. They preserved the bodies of their dead.
- C. They became famous warriors.
- D. They did not preserve the bodies of their dead.

_____ 11. The Egyptian pyramids were
- A. government office buildings.
- B. empty monuments.
- C. tombs for dead pharaohs.
- D. museums.

_____ 12. India's northern border is
- A. the Himalayas.
- B. Sri Lanka.
- C. the Indian Ocean.
- D. China.

_____ 13. Archaeologists know that Mohenjo-Daro was carefully planned because
- A. the fertile soil eventually turned into desert.
- B. homes, workshops, and public buildings were organized together.
- C. the city was built on a flat plain.
- D. the city was used for farming and not trade.

Name _____ Date _____ Class _____

The Ancient World Practice Test A (continued)

_____ 14. Society in India is based on
   A. the caste system.   C. avatars.
   B. clans.   D. religion.

_____ 15. Hindus believe in _____, _____ and _____.
   A. reincarnation, nonviolence, a single god
   C. many gods, reincarnation, nonviolence
   B. reincarnation, violence when necessary, many gods
   D. heaven and hell, nonviolence, a single god

_____ 16. Buddhists believe that giving up selfish desires for wealth is
   A. a way to prevent human suffering.   C. unwise.
                                             D. useless.
   B. a way to eventually become wealthy.

_____ 17. The Maurya ruler Asoka thought of his subjects as his
   A. slaves.   C. parents.
   B. enemies.   D. children.

_____ 18. The ancient Chinese people had little knowledge of other civilizations because of the
   A. desire to learn about others.   C. lack of transportation.
   B. of their dislike for travel.   D. mountains and seas that made travel difficult.

_____ 19. In early Chinese society, a person's first responsibility was to
   A. society.   C. the family.
   B. the boss.   D. religion.

© Pearson Education, Inc., publishing as Pearson Prentice Hall. All rights reserved.

The Ancient World Practice Test A (continued)

_____ 20. In China, the most powerful person in an extended family is
   A. the mother.
   B. the strongest.
   C. the wealthiest.
   D. the oldest man.

_____ 21. Confucius hoped for _____ for China.
   A. peace, stability, and prosperity
   B. conquest and new lands
   C. power
   D. rain and good harvests

_____ 22. In ancient Greece, the new middle class of merchants and artisans overthrew tyrants and started
   A. a war.
   B. a time of peace.
   C. a democracy.
   D. a plan to become more wealthy.

_____ 23. Pericles involved more people in democratic government by
   A. asking women to run for office.
   B. giving slaves the right to vote.
   C. paying a salary to public officials.
   D. creating more government positions.

_____ 24. After driving the last Etruscan king from the throne, the Romans decided to have
   A. their own king installed.
   B. no government.
   C. a republic with elected leaders.
   D. a new Etruscan king.

_____ 25. Why were the Romans able to build taller buildings than the Greeks?
   A. They had more slaves.
   B. They developed concrete and were able to make buildings stronger.
   C. They used marble.
   D. They had a bigger government and more money.

Name _____ Date _____ Class _____

The Ancient World Practice Test B

Directions: *Read each question and choose the best answer. Then write the letter for the answer you have chosen in each blank.*

_____ 1. In ancient India, the people domesticated elephants for
   A. war.
   B. food.
   C. construction.
   D. plowing fields.

_____ 2. Why is it dangerous to live near a river?
   A. too much boat traffic
   B. earthquakes
   C. bad soil
   D. floods

_____ 3. In Sumer, the people practiced polytheism, or belief in
   A. witchcraft.
   B. no religion.
   C. many gods.
   D. one god.

_____ 4. In their desire for riches, the Babylonians and Assyrians were
   A. kind and persuasive.
   B. skilled warriors.
   C. cooperative.
   D. good merchants.

_____ 5. The Assyrian capital of Nineveh had a great library of
   A. parchment manuscripts.
   B. books.
   C. paper documents on farming.
   D. clay tablets of Sumerian writings.

_____ 6. Cuneiform is
   A. a written language of symbols.
   B. the letters of an alphabet.
   C. an early version of English.
   D. a clay token.

_____ 7. Abraham taught the Israelites
   A. farming.
   B. reading.
   C. trade.
   D. monotheism.

© Pearson Education, Inc., publishing as Pearson Prentice Hall. All rights reserved.

Name _____ Date _____ Class _____

The Ancient World Practice Test B (continued)

_____ 8. The Jews left Judaea in A.D. 135 because
   A. they wanted to visit the rest of the world.
   B. the Romans forced them to leave.
   C. the Greeks forced them to leave.
   D. they wanted to search for wealth.

_____ 9. The Nile was used to transport
   A. diamonds.
   B. trade goods.
   C. oranges.
   D. silk.

_____ 10. The Middle Kingdom of Egypt was
   A. between Upper and Lower Egypt.
   B. midway between the East and West.
   C. the merchant class.
   D. a period of time in Egyptian history.

_____ 11. The falcon god Horus was worshipped
   A. everywhere in Egypt.
   B. just in small towns.
   C. only in farming areas.
   D. only in Upper Egypt.

_____ 12. The ancient Egyptian system of writing is called
   A. cuneiform.
   B. alphabet.
   C. symbols.
   D. hieroglyphs.

_____ 13. Aryan warriors from Central Asia invaded and conquered northern India by using
   A. elephants.
   B. chariots.
   C. large armies.
   D. bows and arrows.

_____ 14. According to the ancient caste system, _____ could change castes, because _____.
   A. successful people, newly wealthy people were allowed to move to a higher caste.
   B. bankrupt people, people who lost their business or their farm were forced into a lower caste.
   C. young adults, caste placement was according to a person's occupation.
   D. no one, everyone had to stay in the caste of their parents.

© Pearson Education, Inc., publishing as Pearson Prentice Hall. All rights reserved.

Name _____ Date _____ Class _____

The Ancient World Practice Test B (continued)

_____ 15. Hindus believe that their god Brahma was born from
   A. a golden flower.   C. a golden egg.
   B. a fig tree.   D. the god Vishnu.

_____ 16. Reincarnation means
   A. rebirth of the soul.   C. going to the afterlife.
   B. rebirth of the same body. D. going to heaven.

_____ 17. Siddhartha Gautama is believed to be the founder of what religion?
   A. Hinduism   C. Reincarnation
   B. Islam   D. Buddhism

_____ 18. According to both Buddhism and Hinduism, it is
   A. wrong to harm other living creatures.   C. acceptable to kill animals for food.
   B. wrong to work for a living.   D. acceptable to live just for pleasure.

_____ 19. The Chinese people called the Huang River China's Sorrow because it was
   A. without fish for most of the year.   C. generally thought of as unlucky.
   B. yellow in color and too muddy to bathe.   D. frequently flooded and drowned many people.

_____ 20. After Greece created democracy, slavery
   A. ended.   C. started a great war.
   B. continued.   D. was often debated.

© Pearson Education, Inc., publishing as Pearson Prentice Hall. All rights reserved.

Name _____ Date _____ Class _____

The Ancient World Practice Test B (continued)

Directions: *Read each question and write your answer on the lines provided.*

21. Why did most ancient civilizations develop near rivers?

_____
_____
_____
_____

22. According to Confucius, how should princes and other people who are in power behave?

_____
_____
_____
_____

23. How did the city of Sparta differ from the city of Athens?

_____
_____
_____
_____

24. Why did Roman officials view early Christians as enemies of the empire?

_____
_____
_____
_____

The Ancient World Practice Test C

Directions: *Read each question and choose the best answer. Then write the letter for the answer you have chosen in each blank.*

_____ 1. When modern Europeans found the frozen Iceman in the Alps, how did they know that he had lived about 5,000 years ago?

    A. his copper axe

    B. his finely stitched clothing

    C. his facial features

    D. the letters from his family

_____ 2. The first time people used fire was

    A. in ancient Mesopotamia.

    B. unknown.

    C. in the New Stone Age.

    D. in the Middle Kingdom.

_____ 3. How do we know that religion was important to the ancient Sumerian people?

    A. Their religious books were discovered.

    B. Descendents of the ancient Sumerians still worship the same gods.

    C. Large temples with prayer figures were located in the heart of their cities.

    D. The ancient Sumerians were not religious people.

_____ 4. What does the expression "an eye for an eye" mean in relation to Hammurabi's Code?

    A. Everyone would face the same punishment for the same crime.

    B. If a person accidentally broke the law, it was forgivable.

    C. The punishment for all crimes should be blindness.

    D. The punishment should fit the crime.

_____ 5. Judaism, Christianity, and Islam are

    A. basically the same religion with three different titles.

    B. originally from the same region, but totally different in moral point of view.

    C. three separate religions with nothing in common.

    D. related to one another and share the same moral point of view.

© Pearson Education, Inc., publishing as Pearson Prentice Hall. All rights reserved.

The Ancient World Practice Test C (continued)

_____ 6. People could not travel the entire length of the Nile because
   A. hostile enemies patrolled the water.
   B. a great dam was built across the river.
   C. cataracts, waterfalls, and rapids made it too dangerous.
   D. because it was too long to travel in one lifetime.

_____ 7. Egyptians predicted when the Nile would flood by using
   A. oracles.
   B. astrology.
   C. astronomy.
   D. herbalism.

_____ 8. The Indian city of Mohenjo-Daro had a drainage system made up of
   A. clay pipes above the streets.
   B. clay pipes under the streets.
   C. terraces.
   D. water towers.

_____ 9. Hinduism developed over 3,500 years and absorbed many different beliefs. Hindus believe that
   A. they have the only true religion.
   B. that their founder was an avatar, or a god in human form.
   C. there is only one god.
   D. since people are different, they need many different ways of approaching god.

_____ 10. Buddhism began when Siddhartha Gautama
   A. meditated.
   B. traveled to nirvana.
   C. left India.
   D. joined a monastery.

_____ 11. The Chinese system of using the family name first symbolizes
   A. the importance of the father's family.
   B. the importance of marriage.
   C. that children are not important.
   D. the importance of the family.

_____ 12. What was one way in which Pericles strengthened democracy?
   A. He opened a school to teach democratic policies.
   B. He required Athens to pay a salary to its officials. This allowed poor citizens to hold office.
   C. He outlawed the belief in the gods in order to emphasize education.
   D. He opposed those who sentenced Socrates to death.

© Pearson Education, Inc., publishing as Pearson Prentice Hall. All rights reserved.

Name _____ Date _____ Class _____

The Ancient World Practice Test C (continued)

Directions: *Read each question and write your answer on the lines provided.*

13. Explain how the climate and physical geography of Egypt helped to shape people's lives. Give examples.

   _____
   _____
   _____
   _____
   _____
   _____
   _____

14. Think about ancient India's caste system. How would living in a caste system be different from the way you live today? Give examples.

   _____
   _____
   _____
   _____
   _____
   _____
   _____

15. Briefly explain the problems the Romans faced holding onto their huge empire. What led to their downfall?

   _____
   _____
   _____
   _____
   _____
   _____
   _____

Name _____ Date _____ Class _____

The Ancient World Practice Test C (continued)

16. Religion has had a strong impact on the history and culture of many people. Choose one of the three regions listed below. Then write a short, three-paragraph essay that considers in what way religion has shaped the culture and history of that region. Provide examples to support your points.

Egypt
India
Rome

Name _____ Date _____ Class _____

Asia and the Pacific Practice Test A

Directions: *Read each question and choose the best answer. Then write the letter for the answer you have chosen in each blank.*

_____ 1. Unlike the other countries of East Asia, only China and Mongolia have
   A. wide plains and plateaus.   C. mountains.
   B. long rivers.   D. coasts.

_____ 2. What has a very strong influence on the climates of East Asia?
   A. monsoons   C. forests
   B. earthquakes   D. volcanoes

_____ 3. About 40 million years ago, the Indian subcontinent collided with Asia and formed the
   A. Bay of Bengal.   C. Himalayas.
   B. Indus River.   D. Indian Ocean.

_____ 4. The largest oil-producing region in the world is
   A. Central Asia.   C. Southwest Asia.
   B. Africa.   D. East Asia.

_____ 5. Because large areas of South and Southeast Asia have a tropical climate, what resource is found there?
   A. copper   C. rain forests
   B. wheat   D. oil

_____ 6. Why are many of the native plants and animals in Australia and New Zealand unique?
   A. Plants and animals in Australia and New Zealand have close ties to those in Africa.
   B. Australia and New Zealand are far from other continents.
   C. Australia and New Zealand get more rainfall than any other place in the world.
   D. Australia and New Zealand came out of the Ice Age later than other continents.

_____ 7. In both Australia and New Zealand, most people live in
   A. coastal cities.   C. mountain passes.
   B. river valleys.   D. inland cities.

© Pearson Education, Inc., publishing as Pearson Prentice Hall. All rights reserved.

Asia and the Pacific Practice Test A (continued)

_____ 8. The three major areas of the Pacific island region are Melanesia, Micronesia, and
   A. New Zealand.
   B. Australia.
   C. Tasmania.
   D. Polynesia.

_____ 9. While high islands in the Pacific island region have fertile soil, the soil in the low islands is often
   A. smothered by tiny sea creatures.
   B. poor and sandy.
   C. fertile as well.
   D. ruined by pollution.

_____ 10. Which ancient East Asian culture invented the magnetic compass, the printing press, and silk weaving?
   A. Mongolian
   B. Chinese
   C. North Korean
   D. South Korean

_____ 11. From ancient times until the early 1900s, China was ruled by a series of
   A. councils.
   B. Korean kings.
   C. dynasties.
   D. shoguns.

_____ 12. Why were India and Pakistan partitioned in 1947?
   A. conflict over language differences
   B. geographic barriers formed national borders
   C. conflict over religious differences
   D. the economy of both was strong when separated

_____ 13. The Silk Road influenced the culture of the people of Central Asia by bringing them into contact with people
   A. from East Asia, Southwest Asia, and Europe.
   B. from Africa.
   C. from North America.
   D. from South America.

Asia and the Pacific Practice Test A (continued)

_____ 14. Why did a variety of different cultures develop in Southeast Asia?
   A. The mountains in the region kept groups of people apart from one another.
   B. Many countries invaded the area.
   C. People easily communicated with those who lived outside their own valley.
   D. Many people from the region traveled throughout Europe.

_____ 15. What continent did the Aborigines of Australia and the Maori of New Zealand originally come from?
   A. South America
   B. Europe
   C. Africa
   D. Asia

_____ 16. Which European country took control of both Australia and New Zealand?
   A. France
   B. Italy
   C. Germany
   D. Great Britain

_____ 17. Where did the Chinese Nationalists establish the Republic of China after fleeing mainland China?
   A. Tibet
   B. Taiwan
   C. Mongolia
   D. South Korea

_____ 18. The economy of North Korea is based on
   A. free enterprise.
   B. diversity.
   C. government owned business.
   D. the South Korean economy.

_____ 19. Which landform makes up the southern half of Israel?
   A. the Negev Desert
   B. the Jordan River
   C. the Sahara Desert
   D. the Dead Sea

Name _____ Date _____ Class _____

Asia and the Pacific Practice Test A (continued)

_____ 20. Muslims making the hajj travel to which city?
   A. Riyadh
   B. Jerusalem
   C. Mecca
   D. Babylon

_____ 21. The country that exports more petroleum than any other country on Earth is
   A. Israel.
   B. Saudi Arabia.
   C. Kazakhstan.
   D. Syria.

_____ 22. What is a key economic activity for the Stans (including Afghanistan, Kazakhstan, and Uzbekistan) in Central Asia?
   A. tourism
   B. manufacturing
   C. developing technology
   D. farming

_____ 23. The United States thought that a Communist victory in one country would cause other countries in Southeast Asia to fall to communism. This belief was called the
   A. communism theory.
   B. domino theory.
   C. conspiracy theory.
   D. civil war theory.

_____ 24. What was the result of the Vietnam War?
   A. The United States defeated the North Vietnamese.
   B. The United States and France defeated the North Vietnamese.
   C. The United States pulled out of the war, and North Vietnam conquered South Vietnam.
   D. The United States pulled out of the war, and South Vietnam conquered North Vietnam.

_____ 25. How has life changed for Australia's Aborigines?
   A. Schools now teach Aboriginal languages.
   B. They've gained back all of their ancestral land.
   C. They're no longer allowed to hold cultural events.
   D. Aborigines no longer have a say in Australia's government.

© Pearson Education, Inc., publishing as Pearson Prentice Hall. All rights reserved.

Name _____ Date _____ Class _____

Asia and the Pacific Practice Test B

Directions: *Read each question and choose the best answer. Then write the letter for the answer you have chosen in each blank.*

_____ 1. The Himalayas, the Plateau of Tibet, and the North China Plain are three major landforms in
   A. South Asia.
   B. Central Asia.
   C. East Asia.
   D. Southeast Asia.

_____ 2. The North China Plain, located around the Huang River, is good for farming because
   A. it is windy.
   B. it is mostly desert.
   C. it has rich deposits of loess.
   D. there are few people there.

_____ 3. Because mountains and plateaus cover so much of East Asia, people must farm
   A. only the most fertile land.
   B. only the land that is near the rivers.
   C. every bit of available land.
   D. only the land in the small villages.

_____ 4. The single most important factor that affects the climate of South Asia is
   A. the Himalayas.
   B. the monsoons.
   C. the Ghat Mountains.
   D. the Bay of Bengal.

_____ 5. The largest all-sand desert in the world, the Rub' al-Khali, stretches across
   A. the Arabian Peninsula.
   B. Southeast Asia.
   C. North Africa.
   D. South Africa.

_____ 6. The nations of Cambodia, Laos, Malaysia, Myanmar, Thailand, and Vietnam form
   A. island Southeast Asia.
   B. South Asia.
   C. the Indian subcontinent.
   D. mainland Southeast Asia.

_____ 7. In both Australia and New Zealand, most people live in
   A. coastal cities.
   B. river valleys.
   C. mountain passes.
   D. inland cities.

Asia and the Pacific Practice Test B (continued)

_____ 8. Some of ancient China's most important inventions were paper, gunpowder, and
   A. the printing press.
   B. armored warships.
   C. pottery.
   D. hot-air heating of homes.

_____ 9. Why did Commodore Matthew Perry come to Japan in 1853?
   A. to conquer the country
   B. to overthrow the emperor
   C. to establish American settlements
   D. to force the country to grant trading rights to the United States

_____ 10. When the Communist government came to power in China in 1949, one major change it made in the Chinese way of life was
   A. encouraging the idea of large families.
   B. encouraging women to stop working.
   C. creating farm communes.
   D. establishing private ownership of land.

_____ 11. Why is the environment an important issue for Kazakhstan?
   A. The landfills are full, and recycling plants have not yet been constructed.
   B. The Soviet Union had conducted nuclear tests in the region and left the area with severe radiation pollution.
   C. Tourism, which is a huge part of the country's economy, has dropped due to pollution.
   D. The country receives foreign aid based on how well it looks after the environment.

_____ 12. One of the most important accomplishments of the early Mesopotamians was
   A. the invention of paper.
   B. the invention of the spinning wheel.
   C. the use of silk weaving.
   D. the development of Hammurabi's code of law.

_____ 13. After the Russian Communists formed the Soviet Union, how did the life of nomads in Central Asia change?
   A. Nomads lived on collective farms and could not practice their religion.
   B. Nomads were forced to join the Soviet military.
   C. Nomads were forced to practice Buddhism and pay high taxes to the state.
   D. Nomads were sent to Siberia to work building railroads.

Asia and the Pacific Practice Test B (continued)

_____ 14. Which place did the British found as a penal colony for people convicted of crimes?
- A. Australia
- B. New Zealand
- C. Tahiti
- D. Fiji

_____ 15. Why did moderate Chinese leaders decide to allow some free enterprise in the late 1900s?
- A. to cut cultural ties with the past
- B. to control land use in rural areas
- C. to decrease environmental pollution
- D. to increase economic growth

_____ 16. What is one measure some Japanese companies took to overcome economic recession?
- A. They asked their employees to work shorter hours than Western workers.
- B. They gave their employees longer vacations.
- C. They began to give benefits only to those workers who had performed the best.
- D. They began laying off employees.

_____ 17. What is the main reason that North and South Korea remain divided?
- A. They have different cultural heritages.
- B. The do not speak the same language.
- C. They have political differences.
- D. They have economic differences.

_____ 18. In the 1930s, the lives of Saudi Arabian citizens changed permanently because of
- A. war with Israel.
- B. the collapse of the government.
- C. invasion by the Chinese.
- D. the discovery of oil.

_____ 19. What is produced on an Australian station?
- A. kiwi fruit
- B. transportation
- C. lamb, mutton, beef, and wool
- D. coconut palm, bananas, and sugar cane

_____ 20. The main goal of Aborigines is to
- A. fit into Australian society.
- B. create rock paintings.
- C. gain political office.
- D. regain their ancestral lands.

Name _____ Date _____ Class _____

Asia and the Pacific Practice Test B (continued)

Directions: *Read each question and write your answer on the lines provided.*

21. Compare and contrast the physical geography of Australia and New Zealand. In what ways are Australia and New Zealand similar? In what ways are they different?

    _____
    _____
    _____
    _____

22. Describe briefly the conflict between India and Pakistan. How did it begin? What is the current state of the conflict?

    _____
    _____
    _____
    _____

23. What role does the production of oil play in the economy of Southwest Asia? How does oil affect the people in these countries?

    _____
    _____
    _____
    _____

24. Discuss briefly the changes that Vietnam has seen in the years after the Vietnam War.

    _____
    _____
    _____
    _____

Name _____ Date _____ Class _____

Asia and the Pacific Practice Test C

Directions: *Read each question and choose the best answer. Then write the letter for the answer you have chosen in each blank.*

_____ 1. Where do most of Japan's people live?
   A. in inland rural areas
   B. in rural areas near the coast
   C. in cities near the coast
   D. outside of Japan

_____ 2. How do the Himalayas affect the weather during the winter months in South Asia?
   A. They block the bitter cold air from reaching the region.
   B. They cause heavy rains throughout the region.
   C. They create extremely hot weather throughout the region.
   D. They allow the dry, cold air to reach the region.

_____ 3. Why is the Aral Sea drying up?
   A. The Soviet Union channeled water from the rivers that fed the sea to irrigate crops.
   B. The Aral Sea is actually a salt lake.
   C. The water drains out into too many rivers.
   D. Unusually high temperatures over the last 10 years are causing water to evaporate rapidly.

_____ 4. What is the relationship between petroleum production in Southwest Asia and the people's standard of living there?
   A. All the countries have the same high standard of living.
   B. Countries with oil reserves have higher standards of living than countries without oil reserves.
   C. Countries that import oil have a higher standard of living than other countries.
   D. Countries that export oil have a lower standard of living than other countries.

_____ 5. Where in Asia are the Rub' al-Khali desert, the Euphrates River, and the Kirghiz Steppe?
   A. South and Southeast Asia
   B. East Asia
   C. Southwest and Central Asia
   D. Australia and New Zealand

© Pearson Education, Inc., publishing as Pearson Prentice Hall. All rights reserved.

Asia and the Pacific Practice Test C (continued)

_____ 6. What was the original purpose of the Great Wall of China?
   A. to serve as a border crossing between China and Russia
   B. to keep the people of southern China from escaping northward
   C. to protect China from enemies and nomads in the north
   D. to serve as a barrier between warring states

_____ 7. What are the three main religions of Southeast Asia?
   A. Christianity, Islam, and Buddhism
   B. Hinduism, Buddhism, and Christianity
   C. Hinduism, Buddhism, and Islam
   D. Christianity, Islam, and Hinduism

_____ 8. One effect that the Aryan invasion had on the culture of northern India was introducing
   A. a democratic form of government.
   B. Islam to the area.
   C. the caste system.
   D. laws requiring people to treat one another with humanity.

_____ 9. In which ancient civilization did the people develop a system of writing, produce ideas about law, and irrigate their fields?
   A. Egypt
   B. Mesopotamia
   C. Syria
   D. China

_____ 10. How has South Korea's economy changed since the end of World War II?
   A. It has changed from a farming to an industrial economy.
   B. It has focused on the development of its many natural resources.
   C. It has changed from an industrial to an agricultural economy.
   D. It has stopped importing raw materials for its industries.

_____ 11. While Australia's east coast has fertile farmland, the rest of the country is made up of
   A. semiarid plateaus, desert, and dry grasslands.
   B. mountains and river valleys.
   C. fertile plateaus.
   D. hills and wet grasslands.

Name _____ Date _____ Class _____

Asia and the Pacific Practice Test C (continued)

_____ 12. Australia is one of the world's leading wheat growers, despite the fact that
   A. only a tiny portion of its land is good for farming.
   B. Australia exports no agricultural products.
   C. it has many rivers that frequently flood the land.
   D. few Australians eat wheat products.

Directions: *Read each question and write your answer on the lines provided.*

13. What changes occurred in China after the Communists took power in 1949? Identify both the positive and negative results of these changes.

   _____
   _____
   _____
   _____

14. Compare and contrast Hinduism and Buddhism. How are the two religions similar? How are they different?

   _____
   _____
   _____
   _____

15. Why has the economy of North Korea developed much more slowly than the South Korean economy? What role has government played in each country's economic growth?

   _____
   _____
   _____
   _____
   _____

© Pearson Education, Inc., publishing as Pearson Prentice Hall. All rights reserved.

Name _____ Date _____ Class _____

Asia and the Pacific Practice Test C *(continued)*

16. In a three-paragraph essay, discuss how physical geography and people affect a country's economy. Consider factors such as natural resources and culture and provide several examples from the region of Asia and the Pacific to support your position.

Name _____ Date _____ Class _____

Europe and Russia Practice Test A

Directions: *Read each question and choose the best answer. Then write the letter for the answer you have chosen in each blank.*

_____ 1. What is the population density of Europe like?
   A. Europe has a higher population density than most of the world.
   B. Europe has a lower population density than most of the world.
   C. Europe has almost no population density.
   D. Europe has about the same population density as most of the world.

_____ 2. The North Atlantic Current affects northwestern Europe by bringing
   A. cold water and ice.
   B. stormy weather and snow.
   C. warm water and winds.
   D. strong, dry winds.

_____ 3. Which of the following describes the relative sizes of Europe and Russia?
   A. Europe is a small continent with many countries and Russia is a small country.
   B. Europe is a large continent with many countries and Russia is a small country.
   C. Europe is a large continent with many countries and Russia is a large country.
   D. Europe is a small continent with many countries and Russia is a large country.

_____ 4. Why is Siberia very important to Russia?
   A. It attracts a great deal of tourism.
   B. It has most of Russia's natural resources.
   C. It is the seat of the government.
   D. It is the cultural center of Russia.

_____ 5. Which group of people were Europe's first great philosophers, historians, and writers?
   A. Ancient Greeks
   B. Ancient Romans
   C. Ancient Mayans
   D. Ancient Minoans

_____ 6. During the Middle Ages, society was organized according to a system called
   A. democracy.
   B. dictatorship.
   C. feudalism.
   D. anarchy.

© Pearson Education, Inc., publishing as Pearson Prentice Hall. All rights reserved.

Name _____ Date _____ Class _____

Europe and Russia Practice Test A (continued)

_____ 7. What was the Renaissance?
   A. a shift toward basing science on facts rather than religious beliefs starting in the 1100s
   B. a rebirth of interest in democracy during the 1200s
   C. a shift toward stronger monarchs in Europe in the 1200s
   D. a rebirth of interest in learning and art starting in the 1300s

_____ 8. One important result of the Industrial Revolution was the growth of
   A. small farms.
   B. wages paid to all factory workers.
   C. cities.
   D. family values.

_____ 9. What was an effect of nationalism in Europe during the early 1900s?
   A. Countries learned to work together for the good of all Europe.
   B. Alliances between groups of nations resulted in World War I.
   C. Countries decided to adopt a common currency.
   D. Countries formed a union to protect European political interests.

_____ 10. What happened as a result of the Russian civil war?
   A. Stalin called for a general election.
   B. Lenin created a democratic state.
   C. Lenin created the Union of Soviet Socialist Republics.
   D. The Soviet empire collapsed.

_____ 11. Which war between the United States and Russia lasted from 1945 until 1991?
   A. World War I
   B. the Cold War
   C. World War II
   D. the Russian Revolution

_____ 12. Eastern European cultural traditions such as _____ and _____ brought people together in opposition to the Soviets.
   A. communism, socialism
   B. landforms, waterways
   C. immigration, modernization
   D. language, religion

© Pearson Education, Inc., publishing as Pearson Prentice Hall. All rights reserved.

Europe and Russia Practice Test A (continued)

_____ 13. What happened when Czechoslovakia divided in 1993?
- A. Two new countries were formed peacefully.
- B. Many ethnic groups fought each other.
- C. The Macedonians gained most of the land.
- D. One part of the country joined the Russian Federation.

_____ 14. The largest ethnic group in Russia is the
- A. Mongolians.
- B. Armenians.
- C. Turks.
- D. Slavs.

_____ 15. Which of the following describes the euro?
- A. It is a passport that works in all European countries.
- B. It is the currency used by many European Union members.
- C. It is the measurement of length that will soon replace the meter.
- D. It is the flag for the European Union.

_____ 16. Which of the following statements about British democracy is true?
- A. It grants the king great power.
- B. Its roots go back hundreds of years.
- C. It began after World War II.
- D. It has suffered many civil wars.

_____ 17. One of the current challenges for Sweden's benefit system is in having
- A. a high proportion of retired people who require health care.
- B. citizens who spend too much time working.
- C. citizens who pay the lowest taxes in Europe.
- D. vacations which are too short.

_____ 18. The most important cultural institution in Italy is the
- A. Academy.
- B. Roman Catholic Church.
- C. Parliament.
- D. Communist party.

_____ 19. What happened to Germany at the end of World War II?
- A. It was divided into two countries.
- B. It was reunified.
- C. It joined the European Union.
- D. It was governed by the United Nations.

Europe and Russia Practice Test A (continued)

_____ 20. When immigrants came to France in the 1970s, there was tension because
  A. the country was becoming overcrowded.
  B. it was the first time immigrants were allowed in the country.
  C. immigrant groups fought one another.
  D. the economy was weak and people worried that immigrants would take too many jobs.

_____ 21. What statement best describes life in Moscow?
  A. All the people live as their ancestors did.
  B. No one maintains traditional ways.
  C. The collapse of communism has brought changes to the city, but Russian traditions still remain.
  D. Communism is helping people adapt to new ways.

_____ 22. What statement best describes the war in Bosnia and Herzegovina which began in 1992?
  A. It began when Archduke Ferdinand was assassinated.
  B. People on all sides were mistreated by their enemies.
  C. It started as part of Cold War tensions between the United States and the Soviet Union.
  D. It was a war between Arabs and Jews.

_____ 23. Many people in Ukraine suffered serious health problems because of
  A. the lack of meat and milk in their diet.
  B. the breakdown of the national health system.
  C. the nuclear accident at Chernobyl.
  D. the invasion by Soviet forces.

_____ 24. Immediately after Poland became free from communist control, it changed
  A. environmental standards and began causing widespread pollution.
  B. its language back to a German dialect.
  C. religions, returning to Muslim practices.
  D. it set up a stock market and ended government price controls.

_____ 25. One problem in Russia since the collapse of the Soviet Union has been
  A. constant conflict with China.
  B. oil reserves which are beginning to run out.
  C. a war in Chechnya which has killed tens of thousands of people.
  D. loss of its membership in the United Nations.

© Pearson Education, Inc., publishing as Pearson Prentice Hall. All rights reserved.

Name _____ Date _____ Class _____

Europe and Russia Practice Test B

Directions: *Read each question and choose the best answer. Then write the letter for the answer you have chosen in each blank.*

_____ 1. More than half of Europe is covered by a landform called the
   A. Central Uplands.
   B. Alpine Mountain System.
   C. North European Plain.
   D. Northwestern Highlands.

_____ 2. Western Europe's peninsulas and bays have enabled its countries to become leaders in
   A. culture.
   B. manufacturing.
   C. the mining industry.
   D. the shipping industry.

_____ 3. Two important rivers on the continent of Europe are
   A. the Ural and the Rhine.
   B. the Siberian and the Volga.
   C. the Volga and the Rhine.
   D. the Nile and the Volga.

_____ 4. One of ancient Rome's greatest contributions to the world was
   A. the concept of democracy.
   B. the idea of separate city-states.
   C. an organized system of written laws.
   D. a scientific way of gathering knowledge.

_____ 5. During the Renaissance, Europeans explored new worlds in order to
   A. expand their wealth through trade.
   B. spread democracy.
   C. find places where people could move because their countries were overcrowded.
   D. test their new inventions and manufacturing machines.

_____ 6. What form of government did Lenin bring to Russia?
   A. absolute monarchy
   B. constitutional monarchy
   C. communist
   D. parliamentary government

_____ 7. How did nationalism affect Europe between 1900 and 1950?
   A. It prevented wars between Eastern and Western Europe.
   B. It helped start the United Nations.
   C. It prevented the United States from gaining more influence there.
   D. It contributed to two World Wars.

© Pearson Education, Inc., publishing as Pearson Prentice Hall. All rights reserved.

Europe and Russia Practice Test B (continued)

_____ 8. What happened during the Cold War?
   A. Tension was high between the Soviets and the United States.
   B. The United States and Russia fought a war in Europe.
   C. Stalin changed the Soviet economy to one more like the United States.
   D. Korea and Vietnam fought against each other.

_____ 9. Feudalism was a system in Europe during the Middle Ages that helped bring
   A. about laws that let landowners own the serfs who worked their land.
   B. order to Europe after the Roman Empire collapsed.
   C. about laws that allowed peasants to farm the land and keep most of their crops.
   D. about the discussion of new ideas, especially ones that differed from the church.

_____ 10. Since World War II, how have population patterns changed in Western Europe?
   A. Large numbers of people have left Western Europe.
   B. Large numbers of people stopped leaving Western Europe.
   C. People have left large cities and moved to farms.
   D. The population has seen very little change.

_____ 11. Although there are many different ethnic groups in Eastern Europe, most are
   A. Slavic and practice the same religion.
   B. Slavic and share the same language.
   C. descendants of Slavs.
   D. Serbs and refuse to change traditional ways.

_____ 12. Which of the following describes one change in Russia after the Soviet Union collapsed?
   A. Everyone began speaking the Russian language again.
   B. The Communist Party became strong again.
   C. People gave up producing art and literature.
   D. People went back to worshipping in their traditional churches.

_____ 13. France is well known for its fashion, arts, and
   A. newspapers.
   B. coal deposits.
   C. automobiles.
   D. cooking.

© Pearson Education, Inc., publishing as Pearson Prentice Hall. All rights reserved.

Europe and Russia Practice Test B (continued)

_____ 14. Which of the following are regions of the United Kingdom?

   A. England, Scotland, Wales, Northern Ireland
   B. England, Wales, Northern Ireland, Iceland
   C. England, Scotland, Southern Ireland, Northern Ireland
   D. England, Wales, Northern Ireland, Denmark

_____ 15. Compared to northern Italy, southern Italy is very

   A. wealthy and fashionable.
   B. modern and industrial.
   C. rural and agricultural.
   D. mountainous and dry.

_____ 16. Since reunification, Germany has moved

   A. the capital back to Bonn from Berlin.
   B. the capital back to Berlin from Bonn.
   C. all of the production of consumer goods to the east.
   D. all of the production of consumer goods to the west.

_____ 17. Throughout its history, Ukraine's location and natural resources have attracted

   A. investors.
   B. invaders.
   C. merchants.
   D. shipping experts.

_____ 18. Which statement best describes life in Siberia today?

   A. Life in many Siberian villages is similar to life in American suburbs.
   B. Life in many Siberian villages is still very traditional.
   C. Life in Siberian villages has been changed by capitalism.
   D. Life in Siberian villages is similar to life in Moscow.

_____ 19. Why was the year 1989 so important in Eastern Europe?

   A. Communism began to crumble in the Soviet Union and Eastern Europe.
   B. Sarajevo held the Winter Olympics for the first time.
   C. The Russian Federation was formed.
   D. All of its countries were welcomed into the European Union.

_____ 20. After World War II, Yugoslavia became

   A. several small countries, including Serbia and Croatia.
   B. a democracy under Tito.
   C. a communist country under Tito.
   D. divided in half with a democratic west and a communist east.

© Pearson Education, Inc., publishing as Pearson Prentice Hall. All rights reserved.

Name _____ Date _____ Class _____

Europe and Russia Practice Test B (continued)

Directions: *Read each question and write your answer on the lines provided.*

21. How has Russia's climate affected the development and use of its waterways in the economy?

    _____
    _____
    _____
    _____

22. Briefly describe the living and working conditions for factory workers during the early years of the Industrial Revolution.

    _____
    _____
    _____
    _____

23. Describe the basic differences in the process and the results of the breakup of Czechoslovakia and Yugoslavia. Include reasons why they were so different.

    _____
    _____
    _____
    _____

24. What are conditions like in the area around Chernobyl since the nuclear accident in 1986?

    _____
    _____
    _____
    _____

© Pearson Education, Inc., publishing as Pearson Prentice Hall. All rights reserved.

Name _____ Date _____ Class _____

Europe and Russia Practice Test C

Directions: *Read each question and choose the best answer. Then write the letter for the answer you have chosen in each blank.*

_____ 1. Three vegetation zones shared by Europe and Russia are
- A. forests, grasslands, and tundra.
- B. forests, grasslands, and Mediterranean.
- C. forests, Mediterranean, and tundra.
- D. Mediterranean, grasslands, and tundra.

_____ 2. What is one reason why most of Russia's industry is west of the Ural Mountains?
- A. The natural resources cannot be mined in western Russia.
- B. The Siberian rivers flow toward Russia's important cities.
- C. The country's fossil fuels are on the continent of Asia.
- D. The country's reserves of iron ore are on the continent of Europe.

_____ 3. What was significant about Roman laws?
- A. It was the first time in history that laws were written down.
- B. They were biased toward the powerful and wealthy.
- C. They eventually protected all citizens, not just the powerful and wealthy.
- D. It was the first completely uncorrupt system of government.

_____ 4. Feudalism was a system in Europe during the Middle Ages that assisted
- A. monks in copying old manuscripts.
- B. in bringing order to Europe after the Roman Empire collapsed.
- C. peasants by allowing them to farm the land and keep most of their crops.
- D. in the development and discussion of new ideas even if they differed from the church.

_____ 5. As a result of the events of Bloody Sunday in Russia, Tsar Nicholas agreed to establish
- A. a Russian congress.
- B. an absolute monarchy.
- C. a free educational system.
- D. an improved legal system.

_____ 6. What is one example of the European Union supporting cultural exchange?
- A. the United Nations
- B. the reunification of Germany
- C. the establishment of the euro
- D. the DEBORA project

© Pearson Education, Inc., publishing as Pearson Prentice Hall. All rights reserved.

Europe and Russia Practice Test C (continued)

_____ 7. Which of the following best describes the Slavic languages?

    A. They were common for years in Eastern Europe but died out.

    B. There are about ten Slavic languages spoken in Eastern Europe.

    C. They are only spoken in the Balkans.

    D. They are the official languages of the European Union but aren't commonly spoken.

_____ 8. Which of the following describes one change in France since World War II?

    A. It joined the European Union but dropped out soon afterward.

    B. Immigrants from France have moved to former colonies.

    C. The language has picked up words from many other cultures.

    D. Architecture is no longer important there.

_____ 9. Which of the following describes current conditions in Sweden?

    A. People pay the lowest taxes in Europe.

    B. Everyone is guaranteed health care, paid vacation, and free education.

    C. Its factories are highly productive.

    D. Its young population allows rapid economic growth.

_____ 10. After Poland became free from communist control, it changed the economic system by

    A. providing guaranteed prices for industrial products.

    B. guaranteeing jobs for people in private businesses.

    C. preventing small businesses from importing so many goods.

    D. welcoming foreign investment and setting up a stock market.

_____ 11. What actions did the Soviet Union take after it took control of Ukraine in 1922?

    A. It used Ukraine's farm products and mineral resources to help the rest of the country.

    B. It neglected Ukraine's economy, and farms and mines were abandoned.

    C. It closed the ports on the Black Sea to prevent foreign influence.

    D. It cleared forests and sold the timber but the land wasn't good for farming.

© Pearson Education, Inc., publishing as Pearson Prentice Hall. All rights reserved.

Europe and Russia Practice Test C (continued)

_____ 12. What has been one negative result of the rapid change in Russia from communism to capitalism?

    A. Fewer people can afford consumer goods or to fix up their homes.

    B. Banks became strong and controlled the money supply.

    C. Corruption and criminal gangs make it hard for people to keep the money they earn.

    D. Most traditional Russian customs have been erased in the cities.

Directions: *Read each question and write your answer on the lines provided.*

13. Briefly describe the effect the invention of the printing press in Germany, around 1450, had on literacy and Renaissance ideas.

_____

_____

_____

14. Why have countries such as the United Kingdom and France become multicultural?

_____

_____

_____

15. Briefly describe the changes in the German government since World War II.

_____

_____

_____

_____

Name _____ Date _____ Class _____

Europe and Russia Practice Test C (continued)

16. At different times in recent history, European countries have formed groups to further particular goals. Write a short, three-paragraph essay that describes the alliances of the early 1900s and the European Union of today, and compare their effects on European life.

Name _____ Date _____ Class _____

Foundations of Geography Practice Test A

Directions: *Read each question and choose the best answer. Then write the letter for the answer you have chosen in each blank.*

_____ 1. What are the two basic questions that geographers try to answer?
   A. Who lives on Earth? Why do they live there?
   B. What are the highest and lowest points on Earth? What are the hottest and coldest places on Earth?
   C. Where are things located? Why are they there?
   D. What are our natural resources? How can we preserve them?

_____ 2. Latitude and longitude are measured
   A. in inches.
   B. in miles.
   C. in altitude.
   D. in degrees.

_____ 3. Geographers group places that share a unifying human or physical feature into
   A. locations.
   B. regions.
   C. hemispheres.
   D. districts.

_____ 4. Which of the following is a problem with all globes?
   A. If they are large enough to be complete and detailed, they are too big to be convenient.
   B. Because they are flat, they always have distortions.
   C. Unless they are hollow, they are too heavy to carry.
   D. They are created by mapmakers, who rely on measurements made on the ground.

_____ 5. If you are using a map to find the distance from one city to another, you will need to use the
   A. compass rose.
   B. scale bar.
   C. key.
   D. legend.

_____ 6. One result of Earth's tilt is that Earth has
   A. winds.
   B. weather.
   C. seasons.
   D. daylight.

_____ 7. Most of Earth's surface is covered by
   A. mountains.
   B. plateaus.
   C. land.
   D. water.

© Pearson Education, Inc., publishing as Pearson Prentice Hall. All rights reserved.

Foundations of Geography Practice Test A (continued)

_____ 8. Which force deep inside Earth constantly reshapes the planet's surface?
   A. heat
   B. air
   C. ice
   D. steam

_____ 9. What is climate?
   A. water that falls to the ground as rain, sleet, hail, or snow
   B. the conditions of the air and sky from day to day
   C. how hot or cold the air is
   D. the average weather in a place over many years

_____ 10. Why can so many kinds of plants grow in a tropical rain forest?
   A. A rain forest has a cool, dry climate.
   B. A rain forest has a long, wet winter.
   C. A rain forest has lots of sunlight, heat, and rain.
   D. A rain forest has a vast tundra.

_____ 11. Population density is the number of people who live in a region divided by
   A. the number of roads in that region.
   B. the number of waterways in that region.
   C. the number of square miles or square kilometers in the region.
   D. the number of people who used to live in that region.

_____ 12. What is urbanization?
   A. the growth of farms
   B. the growth of cities
   C. the growth of suburbs
   D. the decrease in suburban populations

_____ 13. What are the three basic economic questions?
   A. What will be produced? How will it be produced? How much will it cost?
   B. What will be produced? How much will it cost? For whom will it be produced?
   C. What will be produced? How will it be produced? For whom will it be produced?
   D. What will be produced? For what purpose will it be produced? Is it necessary?

© Pearson Education, Inc., publishing as Pearson Prentice Hall. All rights reserved.

Foundations of Geography Practice Test A (continued)

_____ 14. Which of these is a particular problem in developed nations?
- A. lack of food and water
- B. air, land, and water pollution
- C. disease
- D. poor healthcare

_____ 15. States are regions that share a
- A. similar population.
- B. similar climate.
- C. common food supply.
- D. government.

_____ 16. Three important features of a culture are
- A. weather, technology, and writing.
- B. language, values, and religious beliefs.
- C. economy, population growth, and climate.
- D. natural resources, landforms, and climate.

_____ 17. Which of the following is the best definition of *civilizations*?
- A. cultures in which people can make and use tools
- B. cultures in which people have developed control over fire
- C. cultures with fully developed agricultural technology
- D. cultures with cities and the use of writing

_____ 18. What is a society?
- A. a pattern of organized relationships among people
- B. a group of people sharing a culture
- C. a grouping of people based on rank or status
- D. a family that includes several generations

_____ 19. The social unit most responsible for teaching the customs and traditions of a culture is
- A. the family.
- B. the government.
- C. the army.
- D. the capitalists.

Name _____ Date _____ Class _____

Foundations of Geography Practice Test A *(continued)*

_____ 20. What is cultural diffusion?
   A. the movement of people from one culture to another
   B. the process of trading goods and services
   C. the process of accepting new ideas and fitting them into a culture
   D. the movement of customs and ideas

_____ 21. Which of the following are renewable resources?
   A. water, coal, wind
   B. water, solar energy, wind
   C. solar energy, wind, oil
   D. wind, water, coal

_____ 22. Why do some people oppose the use of atomic energy?
   A. It uses plentiful materials.
   B. It uses radioactive materials, which can be dangerous.
   C. It causes air pollution.
   D. It uses plant materials, which can cause water pollution.

_____ 23. People who make a living by farming or fishing work in the
   A. first stage of economic activity
   B. second stage of economic activity
   C. third stage of economic activity
   D. highest stage of economic activity

_____ 24. What is industrialization?
   A. a movement of new settlers and their culture to a country
   B. the growth of machine-powered production
   C. the large-scale production of goods by hand or by machine
   D. the use of renewable resources

_____ 25. Which of the following are sources of environmental pollution?
   A. industry, trash, waste recycling
   B. trash, exhaust from cars and trucks, industry
   C. waste recycling, solar energy, industry
   D. exhaust from cars and trucks, waste recycling, trash

© Pearson Education, Inc., publishing as Pearson Prentice Hall. All rights reserved.

Name _____ Date _____ Class _____

Foundations of Geography Practice Test B

Directions: *Read each question and choose the best answer. Then write the letter for the answer you have chosen in each blank.*

_____ 1. Longitude and latitude lines help geographers identify
   A. absolute location.
   B. the depth of oceans.
   C. Earth's distance from the sun.
   D. the height of mountains.

_____ 2. A geographer who explains that "Town A is about 200 miles west of Town B" is giving the
   A. longitude of Town B.
   B. relative location of Town A.
   C. latitude of Town A.
   D. intermediate direction of Town B.

_____ 3. Which of the following statements explains why there are always distortions on a map?
   A. Maps are flat and Earth is round.
   B. Small towns are hard to represent on a map.
   C. Mountains or plains don't show up on a map.
   D. Maps are too small to hold enough information.

_____ 4. What is a compass rose?
   A. a bar that shows how distances on the map compare to actual distances
   B. a flowered pattern used to decorate maps
   C. a diagram of a compass showing directions
   D. a section that explains the symbols and shadings used on a map

_____ 5. What is the difference between weather in low latitudes and weather in high latitudes?
   A. Weather is usually hot in low latitudes and warm in high latitudes.
   B. Weather is usually warm in low latitudes and hot in high latitudes.
   C. Weather is usually cool in low latitudes and warm in high latitudes.
   D. Weather is usually hot in low latitudes and cold in high latitudes.

_____ 6. Why are people able to use only a small part of Earth's fresh water?
   A. Most fresh water is frozen in ice sheets.
   B. Most fresh water has been polluted.
   C. Most fresh water evaporates before it can be used.
   D. Most fresh water is privately owned.

© Pearson Education, Inc., publishing as Pearson Prentice Hall. All rights reserved.

Foundations of Geography Practice Test B (continued)

_____ 7. Earth's climate is affected by latitude, landforms, and a combination of
   A. ice and sand.
   B. wind and water.
   C. ocean depth and sea life.
   D. volcanoes and earthquakes.

_____ 8. What vegetation is found in the tundra?
   A. Grasses and deciduous trees grow in the tundra.
   B. No plants grow in the tundra.
   C. Mosses, grasses, and low shrubs grow in the tundra.
   D. Grasses and coniferous trees grow in the tundra.

_____ 9. One problem faced by the world's population today is
   A. too many jobs.
   B. not enough schools or housing.
   C. a decline in foreign trade.
   D. a decrease in the use of natural resources.

_____ 10. Immigrants to the United States are people who move from
   A. one part of the United States to another part.
   B. the United States to another country.
   C. rural areas in the United States to urban areas in the United States.
   D. other countries to the United States.

_____ 11. Communism, and capitalism are examples of
   A. political systems.
   B. economic systems.
   C. educational methods.
   D. technological achievements.

_____ 12. Which form of government do the United States, Canada, and India have?
   A. direct democracy
   B. representative democracy
   C. constitutional monarchy
   D. absolute monarchy

Name _____ Date _____ Class _____

Foundations of Geography Practice Test B (continued)

_____ 13. Ideas and ways of doing things form a group of people's
  A. cultural traits.
  B. cultural landscape.
  C. cultural institutions.
  D. cultural bonds.

_____ 14. An extended family includes
  A. only parents and their children.
  B. only one or two generations.
  C. brothers, sisters, and cousins of about the same age.
  D. several generations.

_____ 15. Religion is an important part of every
  A. state.
  B. culture.
  C. family.
  D. population.

_____ 16. The process of accepting new ideas and fitting them into a culture is
  A. cultural diffusion.
  B. acculturation.
  C. cultural trait formation.
  D. transformation.

_____ 17. Many living resources, such as trees and food crops, are
  A. renewable.
  B. nonrenewable.
  C. recyclable.
  D. non-recyclable.

_____ 18. The increasing spread of cities and suburbs is called
  A. colonization.
  B. deforestation.
  C. spread.
  D. sprawl.

_____ 19. Which economic activities have an impact on the environment?
  A. only first-level activities
  B. only third-level activities
  C. first-, second-, and third-level activities
  D. first- and third-level activities

_____ 20. Which of the following is one of the greatest challenges of our time?
  A. finding new sources of pollution
  B. identifying renewable resources
  C. finding solutions to environmental problems
  D. developing new designs for hybrid cars

© Pearson Education, Inc., publishing as Pearson Prentice Hall. All rights reserved.

Name _____ Date _____ Class _____

Foundations of Geography Practice Test B (continued)

Directions: *Read each question and write your answer on the lines provided.*

21. What are the five themes geographers use to organize information about Earth and its people?

    _____
    _____
    _____
    _____

22. Why does the sun appear to rise and set on Earth?

    _____
    _____
    _____
    _____

23. What problems are associated with the rapid growth of populations on Earth?

    _____
    _____
    _____
    _____

24. What is deforestation? What other problem is associated with deforestation?

    _____
    _____
    _____
    _____

Name _____ Date _____ Class _____

Foundations of Geography Practice Test C

Directions: *Read each question and choose the best answer. Then write the letter for the answer you have chosen in each blank.*

_____ 1. How is an aerial photograph of Earth's surface similar to a flat map?
- A. Both show details of everything on Earth's surface.
- B. Both are primarily blue and green.
- C. Both give a distorted view of Earth's surface.
- D. Both include historical details.

_____ 2. How does Earth's movement create day and night?
- A. Earth's movement causes clouds to cover the sun.
- B. One revolution of Earth completes one day and one night on Earth.
- C. One rotation of Earth creates day when a region faces the sun and night when it faces away from the sun.
- D. As Earth tilts toward the moon, it creates day, and as the Earth tilts away from the moon, it creates night.

_____ 3. How is climate different from weather?
- A. Climate is how hot or cold the air feels, and weather is the air patterns that flow over Earth.
- B. Weather is precipitation, and climate is temperature.
- C. Weather describes day-to-day changes in the air, and climate is the average weather over many years.
- D. Climate is precipitation, and weather is how hot or cold the air feels.

_____ 4. Why are winds and water so important to Earth's survival?
- A. They create storms that maintain the climates.
- B. They work together so that Earth does not overheat.
- C. They help replenish nonrenewable resources of Earth.
- D. They make sure the air moves in a north-south direction.

_____ 5. Which of the following developments has increased the world's population in the last one hundred years?
- A. advances in medicine and health
- B. higher death rate than birthrate
- C. famine in developing countries
- D. improvements in physical education

© Pearson Education, Inc., publishing as Pearson Prentice Hall. All rights reserved.

Foundations of Geography Practice Test C (continued)

_____ 6. What is one similarity between an absolute monarchy and a dictatorship?
   A. Both have leaders who inherit the right to rule.
   B. Both have leaders with complete, or nearly complete, control over the country.
   C. Both have leaders who are elected by popular vote.
   D. Both involve rule by a very small group of leaders.

_____ 7. What change took place during the Agricultural Revolution?
   A. People began to rely on farming for most of their food.
   B. People began to rely on hunting for most of their food.
   C. People began to use power-driven machinery.
   D. People began to use hand tools.

_____ 8. The family is the basic, most important social unit of
   A. societies in North America.
   B. societies in Africa.
   C. societies in Asia.
   D. all societies.

_____ 9. Which of the following changes affect culture?
   A. changes in the natural environment, technology, and ideas
   B. changes in technology and ideas
   C. changes in the natural environment
   D. none of the above

_____ 10. What is the difference between recyclable resources and renewable resources?
   A. Recyclable resources recycle naturally in the environment, and renewable resources can be replaced.
   B. Renewable resources recycle naturally in the environment, and recyclable resources can be replaced.
   C. Renewable resources cannot be replaced, but recyclable resources can be recreated.
   D. Recyclable resources can be recovered and processed for reuse, whereas renewable resources can be replaced.

Foundations of Geography Practice Test C *(continued)*

_____ 11. Why are many problems associated with energy as a natural resource?

  A. No country has enough energy.
  B. Energy resources are scarce and are not spread evenly around the world.
  C. Most of our energy resources have already been exhausted.
  D. People cannot find energy resources other than fossil fuels.

_____ 12. Which of the following statements best explains the relationship between culture and landscape?

  A. Environment shapes culture, and culture shapes the landscape.
  B. Environment does not affect culture, but culture shapes the landscape.
  C. Environment shapes culture, but culture does not affect the landscape.
  D. In general, there is no relationship between culture and landscape.

Directions: *Read each question and write your answer on the lines provided.*

13. What are two features found on all maps? How are they used?

    _____
    _____
    _____
    _____

14. What is the difference between weathering and erosion? What is the effect of the two processes?

    _____
    _____
    _____
    _____

15. What is the difference between developed countries and developing countries? What kinds of problems do both countries face?

    _____
    _____
    _____
    _____
    _____

Name _____ Date _____ Class _____

Foundations of Geography Practice Test C (continued)

16. What are the three levels of economic activity? Explain how each level of activity contributes to the sale of a fresh ocean fish in a grocery store located inland.

_____
_____
_____
_____
_____
_____
_____
_____
_____
_____
_____
_____
_____
_____
_____
_____
_____
_____
_____
_____
_____
_____
_____
_____

Name _____ Date _____ Class _____

Latin America Practice Test A

Directions: *Read each question and choose the best answer. Then write the letter for the answer you have chosen in each blank.*

_____ 1. The whole of Latin America is located in the
- **A.** Northern Hemisphere.
- **B.** Southern Hemisphere.
- **C.** Western Hemisphere.
- **D.** Eastern Hemisphere.

_____ 2. Which of the following is a long, narrow country in South America?
- **A.** Argentina
- **B.** Chile
- **C.** Suriname
- **D.** Belize

_____ 3. The long mountain chain that runs along the side of South America is called the
- **A.** Rockies.
- **B.** Sierra Nevada.
- **C.** Andes.
- **D.** Sierra Madre.

_____ 4. The Amazon River Basin is home to
- **A.** the rolling highlands called pampas.
- **B.** South America's gauchos.
- **C.** the world's biggest volcanoes.
- **D.** the largest tropical rain forest in the world.

_____ 5. The types of crops grown by farmers in the Andes is influenced in large part by
- **A.** frequent hurricanes.
- **B.** government control.
- **C.** elevation.
- **D.** latitude.

Name _____ Date _____ Class _____

Latin America Practice Test A (continued)

_____ 6. The Aztecs built a great civilization in the area now called
   A. Guatemala.
   B. the Andes.
   C. the Valley of Mexico.
   D. the Yucatán Peninsula.

_____ 7. The Line of Demarcation was an imaginary line that divided control of the territory in the Americas between which two countries?
   A. Spain and Portugal
   B. England and France
   C. Incas and Aztecs
   D. Mayas and Spain

_____ 8. How did the Spanish conquest in the 1500s affect many Native Americans?
   A. Their lives improved.
   B. They died from hunger, overwork, and disease.
   C. They joined the Spanish army.
   D. They received farmland.

_____ 9. Two leaders who contributed to independence in South America were
   A. Miguel Hidalgo and José Morales.
   B. José de San Martin and Simón Bolívar.
   C. Touissant L'Ouverture and Hernán Cortés.
   D. Simón Bolivar and Prince Ferdinand.

_____ 10. In Belize, the official language is English, but in most Central American nations the official language is
   A. Portuguese.
   B. Native American.
   C. French.
   D. Spanish.

_____ 11. A main reason why Mexicans and Central Americans emigrate to the United States is to
   A. work in maquiladoras.
   B. move to cities.
   C. find jobs.
   D. escape earthquakes.

_____ 12. One effect of rapid urbanization in Mexico is
   A. an increase in jobs in rural areas.
   B. a shortage of housing.
   C. a decrease in emigration.
   D. an increase in the rural population.

_____ 13. Mexico City's pollution problem is made worse by its
   A. farmland.
   B. mass transit system.
   C. squatters.
   D. geography.

© Pearson Education, Inc., publishing as Pearson Prentice Hall. All rights reserved.

Name _____ Date _____ Class _____

Latin America Practice Test A (continued)

_____ 14. The Panama Canal allows ships to travel between the Pacific Ocean and the
   A. Atlantic Ocean.
   B. Mediterranean Sea.
   C. Indian Ocean.
   D. Gulf of Mexico.

_____ 15. The biggest problem in building the Panama Canal was
   A. free trade tariffs.
   B. disease.
   C. seasickness.
   D. the language barrier.

_____ 16. Cuba was once a colony of
   A. the Soviet Union.
   B. France.
   C. Great Britain.
   D. Spain.

_____ 17. Many Cuban immigrants to the United States settle in the state of
   A. Texas.
   B. California.
   C. Florida.
   D. Illinois.

_____ 18. Haiti is the only nation in the Americas formed
   A. from a successful revolt of enslaved Africans.
   B. with the assistance of the United States.
   C. by democratic leaders who have never been challenged.
   D. by indigenous people.

_____ 19. Although Puerto Ricans are U.S. citizens, they cannot
   A. vote in U.S. presidential elections.
   B. freely visit the United States.
   C. have a representative in the U.S. Congress.
   D. serve in the U.S. Army.

© Pearson Education, Inc., publishing as Pearson Prentice Hall. All rights reserved.

Latin America Practice Test A (continued)

_____ 20. The capital of Brazil was moved from the coast to the interior because the government wished to
   A. develop the interior by attracting people to it.
   B. provide services to people living in the rain forest.
   C. move from the flooding and heavy rains that plagued the coast.
   D. move the capital to a location where more people already lived.

_____ 21. The Brazilian government has given permission for some people to clear rain forest lands because
   A. Yanomamo are moving to the cities and so no longer depend on the rain forest.
   B. it would allow airplanes to land, which would make travel to the rain forest possible.
   C. businesses need to mine the rain forest.
   D. farmers need the land to make a living.

_____ 22. The three main geographic regions of Peru are the
   A. sierra, the selva, and the coastal region.
   B. pampas, the rain forest, and the selva.
   C. montas, the rain forest, and the sierra.
   D. sierra, the selva, and the monta.

_____ 23. Chile is the world's largest exporter of
   A. diamonds.
   B. potatoes.
   C. copper.
   D. oil.

_____ 24. In the early 1980s, Venezuela was the richest country in Latin America because of
   A. a booming tourist industry.
   B. vast supplies of oil.
   C. abundant rain forest resources.
   D. thriving agricultural production.

_____ 25. Privatization occurs when
   A. foreign companies move into a country to develop its industries.
   B. the government sells its industries to individuals or private companies.
   C. the military takes control of private companies.
   D. the military drafts people involuntarily.

Name _____ Date _____ Class _____

Latin America Practice Test B

Directions: *Read each question and choose the best answer. Then write the letter for the answer you have chosen in each blank.*

_____ 1. Latin America is divided into the following three regions
   A. South America, North America, and Central America.
   B. Mexico, the Caribbean, and Brazil.
   C. the Western Hemisphere, the Northern Hemisphere, and the Southern Hemisphere.
   D. Mexico and Central America, the Caribbean, and South America.

_____ 2. The Panama Canal is important because it
   A. is the only canal of its kind.
   B. is controlled by Colombia.
   C. allows ships to pass from the Indian Ocean to the Caribbean Sea.
   D. cuts shipping time between the Atlantic and Pacific oceans.

_____ 3. Mexico is rich in
   A. hydroelectric power.
   B. minerals.
   C. uranium.
   D. no natural resource.

_____ 4. Mexican farmers who do not own their own land travel from one area to another working on large farms. They are called
   A. urban workers.
   B. migrant workers.
   C. squatters.
   D. caudillos.

_____ 5. When people in the Caribbean celebrate Carnival
   A. favelas come from miles around.
   B. criollos are served from street stands.
   C. calypso bands play.
   D. maquiladoras gather in the streets.

_____ 6. When the Europeans arrived in Latin America, many indigenous groups
   A. increased sharply in population.
   B. decreased sharply in population.
   C. migrated to other areas.
   D. were taken back to Europe as slaves.

_____ 7. All over Latin America, people are
   A. moving to the pampas.
   B. moving to Peru.
   C. moving to cities.
   D. moving to rural areas.

© Pearson Education, Inc., publishing as Pearson Prentice Hall. All rights reserved.

Latin America Practice Test B (continued)

_____ 8. Which of the following statements describes Puerto Rico?
    A. Puerto Rico is an independent country.
    B. Puerto Rico is a commonwealth of the United States.
    C. Puerto Ricans earn less money than people in other Caribbean countries.
    D. Puerto Ricans earn more than people on the United States mainland.

_____ 9. What factor makes Haiti different from other nations in the Americas?
    A. Haiti is the only communist country in Latin America.
    B. Haiti is the only democracy in Latin America.
    C. Haiti is the only nation in the Americas that successfully overthrew a dictator.
    D. Haiti is the only nation in the Americas formed from a successful revolt of enslaved Africans.

_____ 10. How did the Aztecs solve the problem of having too little farmland?
    A. They invented terrace farming.
    B. They built floating gardens.
    C. They built roads to inland plateaus.
    D. They discovered how to use plows and oxen.

_____ 11. Which of the following was a factor in the conquering of the Aztec empire?
    A. The conquerors had the help of indigenous groups.
    B. The conquerors had cannons and guns, while the Aztecs did not.
    C. The Aztecs believed the conquerors might be gods.
    D. all of the above.

_____ 12. The Incas did not have a written language. The Mayas and Aztecs
    A. also could not communicate in writing.
    B. communicated by using runners.
    C. wrote using quipus.
    D. wrote using hieroglyphics.

_____ 13. In the Caribbean, the following groups were there before Columbus
    A. the Arawaks and the Ciboney.
    B. the Caribs and the Uros.
    C. the Quechua and the Ciboney.
    D. the Uros and the Arawaks.

© Pearson Education, Inc., publishing as Pearson Prentice Hall. All rights reserved.

Latin America Practice Test B (continued)

_____ 14. Why is the destruction of Brazil's rain forest a major concern for people in the United States and Europe?
  A. The rain forest provides fossil fuels.
  B. Rain forest land could be used to solve overcrowding of other countries.
  C. The rain forest provides minerals for industry.
  D. The rain forest produces about one third of the world's oxygen and one fifth of the world's fresh water.

_____ 15. In Guatemala, most of the land is owned by
  A. ladinos.
  B. Spaniards.
  C. Quechua.
  D. Maya.

_____ 16. Most of the people of Haiti make a living
  A. fishing.
  B. mining.
  C. farming.
  D. importing and exporting.

_____ 17. Before Fidel Castro came to power in Cuba
  A. most farm and factory workers earned good wages.
  B. the country had been ruled by many dictators.
  C. Batista ruled Cuba and was trying to be a just leader.
  D. rebel groups tried to prevent Castro from seizing power.

_____ 18. Privatization occurs when
  A. private companies get permission from the government to develop industries.
  B. the military takes control of private companies.
  C. the government buys industries from individuals or private companies.
  D. the government sells its industries to individuals or private companies.

_____ 19. Which statement describes Guatemala's people?
  A. Guatemalans are largely Native Americans.
  B. Guatemalans are largely mestizos.
  C. Native Americans have always controlled most of the land in Guatemala.
  D. Guatemalans are largely European.

_____ 20. When Spain controlled much of Latin America, it allowed
  A. indigenous leaders to help govern.
  B. local cultures to govern certain areas.
  C. the division of the territory into provinces in order to maintain control.
  D. colonial officials to rule with little supervision.

Name _____ Date _____ Class _____

Latin America Practice Test B (continued)

Directions: *Read each question and write your answer on the lines provided.*

21. Briefly describe some of the benefits and drawbacks of life in the cities of Mexico and Central America. What causes the drawbacks?

    _____
    _____
    _____
    _____

22. Identify the ethnic groups of Central America, and explain how these groups came to be there.

    _____
    _____
    _____
    _____

23. Explain how elevation affects climate and vegetation. Give examples of the kinds of crops grown at different elevations in Latin American countries.

    _____
    _____
    _____
    _____

24. What is the danger of having a one-resource economy? Using any one of the Latin American countries you've studied, give an example.

    _____
    _____
    _____
    _____

Name _____ Date _____ Class _____

Latin America Practice Test C

Directions: *Read each question and choose the best answer. Then write the letter for the answer you have chosen in each blank.*

_____ 1. In Latin America, climates near the Equator are most likely
   A. tropical.
   B. semiarid.
   C. Mediterranean.
   D. tundra.

_____ 2. Climate in Latin America is affected by
   A. elevation.
   B. wind patterns.
   C. the Equator.
   D. all of the above.

_____ 3. Volcanoes, plains, plateaus, and mountains are some examples of the _____ in Latin America.
   A. climates
   B. resources
   C. landforms
   D. sectors

_____ 4. Two great civilizations from Middle America were
   A. the Mayas and the Aztecs.
   B. the Incas and the Peruvians.
   C. the Anasazi and the Incas.
   D. the Aztecs and the Uros.

_____ 5. One great achievement of the Incas was their
   A. organized legal code.
   B. strict system of social classes.
   C. writing system.
   D. system of roads and bridges.

_____ 6. Augusto Pinochet Ugarte was
   A. a Catholic priest who defended the rights of the poor in Chile before being elected president.
   B. the winner of the 1988 elections in Chile because he was the only one on the ballot.
   C. removed from office by rebel groups.
   D. the one who led the armed forces and took control of the government in Chile.

_____ 7. In Lima, Peru, Spanish social classes determined
   A. nothing on their own.
   B. where people lived.
   C. whether one would be allowed to work.
   D. one's ancestry.

© Pearson Education, Inc., publishing as Pearson Prentice Hall. All rights reserved.

Latin America Practice Test C (continued)

_____ 8. Artists like Diego Rivera and David Alfaro Siqueiros created
   A. new directions for European art forms.
   B. a new Latin American art form by painting murals on walls.
   C. a revival of an ancient Native American art form.
   D. portraits of the wealthy.

_____ 9. What do French Guiana and Puerto Rico have in common?
   A. They are not independent nations.
   B. They are both commonwealths of the United States.
   C. They are both islands.
   D. Few of their people are of mixed African and European ancestry.

_____ 10. After 1825, only _____ and _____ were ruled by Spain.
   A. Argentina, Columbia
   B. Cuba, Puerto Rico
   C. Venezuela, Colombia
   D. Ecuador, Peru

_____ 11. When Spain controlled much of Latin America, it allowed
   A. indigenous leaders to help govern.
   B. local cultures to govern certain areas.
   C. the division of the territory into provinces to maintain control.
   D. colonial officials to rule with little supervision.

_____ 12. Which of the following statements about the Amazon rain forest is true?
   A. Loss of habitat may destroy rare plants that provide important medicines before they have been discovered.
   B. Since mining and logging have become strictly regulated, they are no longer a threat to the area.
   C. The pollution caused by cutting down too many trees is of great concern to Brazil and its neighbors, but isn't really of any major to concern to anyone living outside South America.
   D. Since opening up the rain forest and enabling more travel, Native American villages in the area have benefited greatly.

Name _____ Date _____ Class _____

Latin America Practice Test C (continued)

Directions: *Read each question and write your answer on the lines provided.*

13. Explain how the distance of a country from the Equator affects climate and vegetation. Give examples of the kinds of crops grown in several countries.

    _____
    _____
    _____
    _____

14. Identify the ethnic groups of the Caribbean, and explain how these groups came to be there.

    _____
    _____
    _____
    _____
    _____
    _____

15. Briefly explain the problems the Mayas in Guatemala have encountered holding onto their land and culture.

    _____
    _____
    _____
    _____
    _____

Name _____ Date _____ Class _____

Latin America Practice Test C (continued)

16. Europeans have had a strong impact on the history of Latin America and its native peoples. Choose either the Aztec or Incan Empire. Write a short, three-paragraph essay that compares what life in the empire may have been like before and after the Europeans arrived. Provide examples to support your points.

Medieval Times to Today Practice Test A

Directions: *Read each question and choose the best answer. Then write the letter for the answer you have chosen in each blank.*

_____ 1. Which of the following describes Byzantine culture?

   A. It was focused strictly on ancient Greek customs and influences.

   B. It was focused strictly on ancient Roman customs and influences.

   C. It was focused strictly on Christian teachings and influences.

   D. It combined ancient Greek and Roman influences as well as Christian influences.

_____ 2. What was God's message as preached by Muhammad?

   A. that all people were brothers and sisters in a community established by God

   B. that they could all grow wealthy from war and trade, but only if they put their faith in God

   C. that God had told Muhammad that he was destined to be king and rule a great empire

   D. that the stories of Adam, Noah, Abraham and Moses should be forgotten

_____ 3. Islam spread after Muhammad's death because

   A. it was a time when Christianity was very weak.

   B. royalty in Europe learned about it.

   C. merchants and traders spread it to other lands and Arab armies conquered new lands.

   D. the people of China were eager to change their religious beliefs.

_____ 4. What was the Bantu migration?

   A. the yearly migration of a now extinct bird in Africa called the Bantu

   B. when a large number of Bantu speaking people migrated across Africa beginning about 2000 B.C.

   C. when the Bantu tribe moved into Saudi Arabia from other parts of the Arabian Peninsula

   D. when all of the Bantu tribe left Africa for Europe about 2,000 years ago

_____ 5. Which of the following was an important source of wealth for ancient Ghana?

   A. salt and gold

   B. the slave trade

   C. agricultural products

   D. trade with China and the Far East

Medieval Times to Today Practice Test A (continued)

_____ 6. Which country conquered many cities on Africa's east coast in 1500s?
   A. Spain
   B. Portugal
   C. Great Britain
   D. France

_____ 7. Which of the following did the Incas use to keep records instead of using a written language?
   A. a complex calendar using stone blocks
   B. a system of colored feathers
   C. carvings in stone walls
   D. a system of knotted strings

_____ 8. Mayans worshipped many gods, including ones symbolizing
   A. rice, sun, and rain.
   B. maize, sun, and rain.
   C. lions, tigers, and birds.
   D. sun, rain, and gold.

_____ 9. Some of the mounds built in North America were used as
   A. military forts.
   B. tombs, but others weren't.
   C. homes for the wealthiest people.
   D. protection against flooding rivers.

_____ 10. One important change in Chinese culture during the Tang dynasty was
   A. the adoption of Confucius' teachings.
   B. the elimination of taxes.
   C. the building of a great network of roads.
   D. the closing of the Silk Road.

_____ 11. In 894, official relations between China and Japan ended when
   A. Kyoto burned.
   B. the war between Asia and India began.
   C. Japan developed its own traditions.
   D. China developed its own traditions.

_____ 12. The social system in the Delhi sultanate in India was built on
   A. equality for all people.
   B. the caliph's decision on where each individual and family belonged.
   C. a caste system which was opposed by the Hindu religion.
   D. a caste system which was supported by the Hindu religion.

_____ 13. Vikings who attacked Europe from about 800 through 1100 came from
   A. areas of Denmark, Sweden, and Norway.
   B. Iceland.
   C. Ireland.
   D. Russia.

© Pearson Education, Inc., publishing as Pearson Prentice Hall. All rights reserved.

Medieval Times to Today Practice Test A (continued)

_____ 14. One reason the Roman Catholic Church was so powerful in Western Europe during the Middle Ages was because
- A. it was very wealthy and owned more land than anyone else.
- B. it offered monetary rewards for people who joined it.
- C. it supported new scientific discoveries.
- D. it supported peasants when they opposed the nobles.

_____ 15. What was the reason for the Crusades?
- A. Constantine wanted to rule a larger empire and needed a reason to attack the Turks.
- B. Muslim Turks were not allowing European pilgrims to travel into Jerusalem.
- C. Muslim warriors had attacked the Vatican and killed the Pope.
- D. European Christians were not allowing Muslim Turks to travel into Jerusalem.

_____ 16. One of the things Martin Luther wanted to reform about the Roman Catholic Church was
- A. the way people were forgiven through confession.
- B. the way priests dressed.
- C. the way cathedrals were designed.
- D. the way it sold indulgences, or pardons for sins.

_____ 17. Where did Columbus think he was when he first landed in the Americas in 1492?
- A. India
- B. China
- C. Africa
- D. Brazil

_____ 18. Who paid most of the taxes in France around the time of Louis XIV?
- A. the nobles
- B. the church
- C. the peasants
- D. the middle class

_____ 19. Which country controlled Central and South America during the 1500s?
- A. Great Britain
- B. France
- C. Spain
- D. Italy

Medieval Times to Today Practice Test A (continued)

_____ 20. John Locke believed that people were basically reasonable and good. He argued that
   A. the scientific method was unnecessary because people were already reasonable.
   B. the Enlightenment was taking too much power away from the Church.
   C. people had natural rights belonging to them from birth.
   D. people could earn special rights and privileges from good deeds they accomplished.

_____ 21. Which country was the first to overthrow and execute its monarch?
   A. France
   B. England
   C. Russia
   D. the Netherlands

_____ 22. Which of the following describes the Industrial Revolution?
   A. It began in France and spread to Great Britain and the United States.
   B. It began in Great Britain and spread to Europe and the United States.
   C. It began in the United States and spread to Europe and Great Britain.
   D. It began in Ireland and spread to Great Britain and the United States.

_____ 23. One result of Napoleon's rule in Europe was
   A. the spread of nationalism.
   B. the total collapse of France when he was defeated.
   C. the idea that a single ruler was the best way to make Europe strong.
   D. the end of military alliances.

_____ 24. Communism promised Russians that
   A. everyone would get to vote for the government they wanted.
   B. everyone would get an equal share of the country's wealth.
   C. Russia would attack its neighbors and conquer them.
   D. they could return to an earlier system of nobles and peasants.

_____ 25. The year 1949 was important in the Cold War because
   A. the Berlin Wall was built.
   B. China attacked Korea.
   C. the Soviets supported the war in Vietnam.
   D. Communists took control in China and the Soviets developed the atomic bomb.

© Pearson Education, Inc., publishing as Pearson Prentice Hall. All rights reserved.

Name _____ Date _____ Class _____

Medieval Times to Today Practice Test B

Directions: *Read each question and choose the best answer. Then write the letter for the answer you have chosen in each blank.*

_____ 1. The Church split into the Roman Catholic and Eastern Orthodox churches in 1054 because
  - A. Constantinople was conquered by Mongols from the east.
  - B. the leaders of their governments were at war.
  - C. people worshipped differently and differed on how much power the pope should have.
  - D. European rulers wanted two popes.

_____ 2. Muslims are called to prayer five times each
  - A. day.
  - B. week.
  - C. month.
  - D. year.

_____ 3. Which of the following did Bantu culture bring to other cultures over the course of their migrations?
  - A. guns and cannons
  - B. the use of gold and salt
  - C. iron tools and crops such as yams
  - D. the use of camels for caravans

_____ 4. When Mansa Musa ruled Mali he
  - A. made Islam the official religion.
  - B. did not collect taxes from traders.
  - C. refused to travel outside of his kingdom.
  - D. forced others to convert to Christianity.

_____ 5. The language of the Swahili people developed
  - A. from their use of picture writing.
  - B. in Central Africa but moved west with their migration.
  - C. in northern Africa and was used by traders on the Mediterranean Sea.
  - D. on the east coast of Africa and is still used today.

_____ 6. One of the things that helped unify the Incan empire was
  - A. their use of iron tools for building.
  - B. a vast network of roads.
  - C. their love of their capital city which was built on a lake.
  - D. flat land which made travel easy.

_____ 7. What is the correct order of Central American civilizations, from earliest to latest?
  - A. Incan, Mayan, Aztec
  - B. Olmec, Aztec, Mayan
  - C. Mayan, Incan, Aztec
  - D. Olmec, Mayan, Aztec

© Pearson Education, Inc., publishing as Pearson Prentice Hall. All rights reserved.

Medieval Times to Today Practice Test B (continued)

_____ 8. Which of the following describes the Plains Indians of North America?
  A. Some were farmers, some hunters, and some did both.
  B. They were all farmers.
  C. They were all hunters.
  D. Many depended on fishing.

_____ 9. The Song dynasty changed the system of government in China by
  A. allowing women to make many government decisions.
  B. holding elections in all of the larger towns.
  C. hiring people with the best ability, not just those of the wealthiest families.
  D. modeling it after European governments.

_____ 10. The samurai in Japan lived by rules that said
  A. they could fight for whoever paid them the most.
  B. writing poetry was the best way to become closer to god.
  C. all western influences were bad.
  D. their honor was more important than money or their life.

_____ 11. During the Middle Ages, nearly all people in Western Europe were
  A. members of the Roman Catholic Church.
  B. living in trading centers.
  C. using money to buy their goods.
  D. not happy with the cathedrals.

_____ 12. Peter the Hermit led a group of crusaders who
  A. captured Jerusalem without much fighting.
  B. were easily defeated by the Turks.
  C. were well-equipped with weapons and supplies.
  D. returned to Europe before they reached the Holy Land.

_____ 13. When the Magna Carta was signed in England in 1215, it required
  A. nobles to swear allegiance to the king or to leave the country.
  B. all nobles to fight in the Hundred Years' War.
  C. the king to consult a council of nobles and clergy before raising taxes.
  D. the king to form a new church which wouldn't recognize the pope's power.

© Pearson Education, Inc., publishing as Pearson Prentice Hall. All rights reserved.

Medieval Times to Today Practice Test B (continued)

_____ 14. How are Leonardo da Vinci and Michelangelo symbols of the Renaissance?
  A. They were very involved with government and royal families.
  B. They didn't allow the church to influence their art.
  C. They only concentrated on creating great art.
  D. They were skilled in many different fields.

_____ 15. Who allowed the Inquisition in order to strengthen the Roman Catholic Church?
  A. Elizabeth I in England
  B. Ferdinand and Isabella in Spain
  C. Peter the Great in Russia
  D. Louis XIV in France

_____ 16. What was similar about how the Aztec and Incan empires were conquered in the 1500s?
  A. Their rulers were kidnapped by Spanish conquistadors.
  B. Neither one fought against Spanish invaders.
  C. Key battles were won by Spanish ships armed with cannons.
  D. Portuguese armies invaded them in a search for gold.

_____ 17. One important issue in the American revolt against the British in 1776 was
  A. whether there should be an absolute monarch in America.
  B. freedom of travel between the countries.
  C. whether the Church in Britain had power in America.
  D. the power to tax people in America without representation in Parliament.

_____ 18. An important principle of the Napoleonic Code was that
  A. kings could only rule if the people approved of them.
  B. all people were equal under the law.
  C. nobles should pay as much in taxes as peasants.
  D. the Church could no longer appoint government officials.

_____ 19. Just before the Great Depression, the United States was
  A. struggling to make its factories more modern.
  B. slowly recovering from World War I.
  C. richer than any country had ever been.
  D. competing against Japan as the strongest economy in the world.

Name _____ Date _____ Class _____

Medieval Times to Today Practice Test B (continued)

_____ 20. In developing nations where many people are poor, large families
   A. can help support the family with many workers and help with care of older parents.
   B. are uncommon because there are too many people to feed.
   C. usually split up and live in different places.
   D. get support from the governments so that more children can go to school.

Directions: *Read each question and write your answer on the lines provided.*

21. Why was the period from about A.D. 800 through 1100 called the Golden Age of Muslim culture? Provide at least two examples.

_____
_____
_____
_____

22. Briefly describe the census used by the Incans and how it was useful.

_____
_____
_____

23. How did the Himalayas affect the early civilizations of the Indian subcontinent?

_____
_____
_____
_____

24. What made exploration of new lands from 1400 to 1600 possible?

_____
_____
_____
_____

© Pearson Education, Inc., publishing as Pearson Prentice Hall. All rights reserved.

Name _____ Date _____ Class _____

Medieval Times to Today Practice Test C

Directions: *Read each question and choose the best answer. Then write the letter for the answer you have chosen in each blank.*

_____ 1. One reason for the accomplishments of the Golden Age of Muslim culture (A.D. 800 through 1100) was
   - **A.** its wealth from trade and the lands it controlled.
   - **B.** the emphasis on Greek and Roman traditions.
   - **C.** its trade and contacts with civilizations to the south of the Sahara desert.
   - **D.** its development of new ships which allowed it to explore new cultures.

_____ 2. Which of the following describes historians' beliefs about the initial reason for the Bantu migration?
   - **A.** A great drought hit northern Africa.
   - **B.** Invaders landed on the western coast of Africa and the Bantu moved east to avoid them.
   - **C.** No one is sure why the migration began.
   - **D.** The Bantus needed farmland to feed their growing population.

_____ 3. Which statement best describes Ethiopia?
   - **A.** Its people speak only one language.
   - **B.** It has been a Muslim nation since the A.D. 600s.
   - **C.** It became Christian in the A.D. 300s.
   - **D.** Its people have always lived in cities rather than in villages or on farms.

_____ 4. The Aztec capital was located on an island in the middle of a lake because
   - **A.** it offered a very good defense against attack.
   - **B.** of a legend concerning their god of war.
   - **C.** it was cooler than the surrounding area in the summer.
   - **D.** it had a good supply of stone for building bridges and roads.

_____ 5. Some of the pueblos of the Anasazi in North America were
   - **A.** five stories high.
   - **B.** built from wood.
   - **C.** just one story high but spread out over hundreds of rooms.
   - **D.** built directly on the banks of powerful rivers.

© Pearson Education, Inc., publishing as Pearson Prentice Hall. All rights reserved.

Medieval Times to Today Practice Test C (continued)

_____ 6. When people in China began using movable type for printing
- A. they shared their discovery with visitors from Europe.
- B. books became much cheaper and knowledge spread more quickly.
- C. the ruling dynasty tried to prevent its use.
- D. they printed the first organized code of laws.

_____ 7. During the Middle Ages, the lord of the manor controlled
- A. few peasants because the Church took over protection of the people.
- B. what protection the king provided.
- C. the lives of the peasants who lived and worked there.
- D. what the Church was allowed to tell the peasants.

_____ 8. One of the major reasons for the Age of Exploration was that European countries wanted
- A. to solve overcrowding.
- B. to share ideas with people from other cultures.
- C. to test their new inventions and scientific theories.
- D. to find new routes for trade which would increase their wealth.

_____ 9. The strong monarchs in Europe during the 1600s and 1700s believed
- A. they needed to share power with their people to be effective.
- B. they were chosen by God and should have absolute power.
- C. that they shouldn't compete with the church for power.
- D. that Europe should be ruled by just one royal family.

_____ 10. Which of the following was an important change during the Industrial Revolution?
- A. Inventors learned how to use steam power instead of water power.
- B. Inventors learned how to use the gasoline engine.
- C. Factories switched from producing consumer goods to processing farm products.
- D. Factories switched from burning coal to using electricity.

Medieval Times to Today Practice Test C (continued)

_____ 11. In Europe during the early 1900s, there were
   A. countries willing to cooperate with each other to strengthen their economies.
   B. major divisions between countries according to their religions.
   C. meetings to determine which countries would control different areas of Latin America.
   D. rivalries, military build-up, and the growth of alliances.

_____ 12. Since World War II, there have been
   A. few changes in the number of countries in the world.
   B. more than fifty new countries created, most of them in Africa.
   C. strong economies growing in Latin America and Africa.
   D. few problems with the environment because countries have worked together against pollution.

Directions: *Read each question and write your answer on the lines provided.*

13. Briefly describe the split in the Muslim religion after A.D. 656 between the Shiites and the Sunnis.

_____
_____
_____
_____

14. Why was the Taj Mahal built and how did it contribute to the collapse of the Mughal empire?

_____
_____
_____
_____

15. Briefly describe the living and working conditions for factory workers during the early years of the Industrial Revolution.

_____
_____
_____
_____

Name _____ Date _____ Class _____

Medieval Times to Today Practice Test C (continued)

16. For about 200 years European armies fought with Muslim armies in the Crusades, which began around 1099. Write a short, three-paragraph essay that describes the reasons for the Crusades and their effects on Europe.

_____
_____
_____
_____
_____
_____
_____
_____
_____
_____
_____
_____
_____
_____
_____
_____
_____
_____
_____
_____
_____
_____
_____
_____
_____

Name _____ Date _____ Class _____

The United States and Canada Practice Test A

Directions: *Read each question and choose the best answer. Then write the letter for the answer you have chosen in each blank.*

_____ 1. The United States and Canada are bordered on the east by
   A. the Pacific Ocean.
   B. the Atlantic Ocean.
   C. Mexico.
   D. the Gulf of Mexico.

_____ 2. The people of the United States and Canada use lakes and rivers for
   A. transportation only.
   B. transportation and recreation only.
   C. recreation and industry.
   D. transportation, recreation, and industry.

_____ 3. Which of these statements best explains why much of Canada is very cold?
   A. Much of Canada lies far from the Equator.
   B. Much of Canada is near an ocean.
   C. Much of Canada is far from an ocean.
   D. Much of Canada is near a mountain range.

_____ 4. A province is a political division of Canada much like
   A. a township in the United States.
   B. a county in the United States.
   C. a state in the United States.
   D. a region in the United States.

_____ 5. How much of the land of Canada is covered in forests?
   A. about 5 percent
   B. almost all
   C. nearly half
   D. none

_____ 6. What was the Louisiana Purchase?
   A. a present from President Lincoln to King Louis and Queen Ana of France
   B. a law passed in 1862 giving free land to anyone willing to farm it for five years
   C. the belief that the United States should own all of North America
   D. the sale of land in North America in 1803 by France to the United States

_____ 7. The framework for the federal government of the United States is
   A. the Declaration of Independence.
   B. the Articles of Confederation.
   C. the Constitution.
   D. the Treaty of Paris.

© Pearson Education, Inc., publishing as Pearson Prentice Hall. All rights reserved.

Name _____ Date _____ Class _____

The United States and Canada Practice Test A (continued)

_____ 8. During the first years of the United States, who was allowed to vote?
   A. All adults were allowed to vote.
   B. All white adults were allowed to vote.
   C. All white male adults were allowed to vote.
   D. All white male adults who owned property were allowed to vote.

_____ 9. Abolitionists were people who believed that
   A. slavery was right.
   B. slavery was wrong.
   C. slavery was not an important issue.
   D. slavery should be extended to Canada.

_____ 10. How did Canada gain its independence from Great Britain?
   A. The Canadian army beat the British in 1776.
   B. In 1982, the king of England granted Canada independence.
   C. Canadians won the War of 1812.
   D. In 1982, Canadians adopted a new constitution.

_____ 11. The Canadian government is modeled on the governmental system of
   A. Great Britain.
   B. the United States.
   C. France.
   D. Germany.

_____ 12. Why are the United States and Canada so culturally diverse?
   A. Immigrants from many countries have contributed to the cultures of both nations.
   B. Neither country has allowed immigration.
   C. The geography of North America made both nations culturally diverse.
   D. Only Canada is culturally diverse.

_____ 13. Most of the treaties that were signed between the United States government and the Native Americans were broken by settlers because
   A. Native Americans wanted to reclaim their lands to the east.
   B. a new warring culture had become popular among Native Americans.
   C. they wanted to continue moving westward.
   D. they wanted to return to eastern cities.

The United States and Canada Practice Test A (continued)

_____ 14. Canada considers itself to be a cultural

  A. melting pot, where immigrants come and adapt to its culture.
  B. puzzle, where different cultures fit together perfectly.
  C. hybrid, where American customs combine with Canadian customs.
  D. mosaic, where separate cultures come to live side by side.

_____ 15. The United States and Canada were both British colonies. What other cultural trait do they share?

  A. Both countries created empires.
  B. They share the same geography and climate.
  C. Both are shaped by immigration.
  D. Slavery led to civil war in both countries.

_____ 16. Many French Canadians want Quebec to become

  A. a separate country.
  B. more active in the national government.
  C. two separate provinces.
  D. joined with surrounding provinces to make one larger province.

_____ 17. The economy of the Northeast United States is based on its

  A. harbors.
  B. farmland.
  C. cities.
  D. recreational areas.

_____ 18. Which of the following is a state in the southern United States?

  A. Pennsylvania
  B. Connecticut
  C. Washington, D.C.
  D. North Carolina

_____ 19. In the Midwest of the United States, family farms are being replaced by

  A. community farms.
  B. corporate farms.
  C. fast food chains.
  D. smaller farms.

_____ 20. Today, people in the West of the United States are working on responsible development, which involves balancing

  A. the interests of farms and cities.
  B. the interests of corporations and business.
  C. the needs of the environment, community, and economy.
  D. the needs of the environment and small towns.

The United States and Canada Practice Test A (continued)

_____ 21. The capital city of Canada, Ottawa, is located in which province?

    A. Ottawa is in Ontario, on the border with Quebec.

    B. Ottawa is in Quebec, on the border with Ontario.

    C. Ottawa is in Quebec, on the border with New Brunswick.

    D. Ottawa is in Saskatchewan, on the border with Manitoba.

_____ 22. During the late 1800s and early 1900s, what did Canada do to encourage people to settle in the Prairie Provinces?

    A. Canada protected the buffalo in the area.

    B. Canada encouraged local indigenous people to farm in the area.

    C. Canada established new cities in the area.

    D. Canada advertised free land in European newspapers.

_____ 23. How did the discovery of gold in British Columbia affect the lives of the indigenous peoples?

    A. The indigenous people sold their minerals and land, and many became rich.

    B. The indigenous people sold goods to the miners, and many became rich.

    C. The indigenous people opened new stores in the boomtowns.

    D. The indigenous people lost their land.

_____ 24. What is an important similarity between British Columbia and the Atlantic Provinces?

    A. Both are relatively close to Europe.

    B. Both are relatively close to Asia.

    C. Both are bordered by ocean.

    D. Both are strongly influenced by the Viking heritage.

_____ 25. How is the government of Canadian territories different from the government of Canadian provinces?

    A. Territories have more control over local concerns than provinces do.

    B. Territories have representatives in the House of Commons, but provinces do not.

    C. Provinces have representatives in the House of Commons, but territories do not.

    D. The federal government exercises more control over the territories than over the provinces.

© Pearson Education, Inc., publishing as Pearson Prentice Hall. All rights reserved.

Name _____ Date _____ Class _____

The United States and Canada Practice Test B

Directions: *Read each question and choose the best answer. Then write the letter for the answer you have chosen in each blank.*

_____ 1. One major landform found in both the United States and Canada is
   A. Mount St. Helens.
   B. the Rocky Mountains.
   C. the Great Basin.
   D. Mount Logan.

_____ 2. Which of the following affects the climate of the United States and Canada?
   A. vegetation
   B. oceans, mountains and distance from the Equator
   C. Vancouver Island
   D. cloud cover

_____ 3. Mixed forests include
   A. pine trees and fir trees.
   B. coniferous trees.
   C. all kinds of deciduous trees.
   D. coniferous trees and deciduous trees.

_____ 4. About what fraction of Canada's land is suitable for farming?
   A. one tenth
   B. one fifth
   C. one fourth
   D. one half

_____ 5. How did the United States acquire the Louisiana Territory?
   A. The United States fought a war against Spain.
   B. The United States fought a war against France.
   C. The United States bought it from France.
   D. The United States simply moved in and claimed the land.

_____ 6. What was the Confederacy?
   A. It was a group of states within the United States.
   B. It was a new country formed by states that withdrew from the United States.
   C. It was an organization of people who opposed slavery.
   D. It was an organization of states that opposed war.

_____ 7. What was the Homestead Act of 1862?
   A. It offered free farming equipment to settlers.
   B. It offered building supplies to settlers.
   C. It offered free houses to settlers.
   D. It offered free land to settlers.

The United States and Canada Practice Test B (continued)

_____ 8. After the American Revolution, why did Great Britain divide Canada into two colonies?

   A. to increase trade between colonies
   B. to avoid problems between Loyalists and French Canadians
   C. to create a place for freed slaves
   D. It created one colony for Native Americans and another for settlers from Europe.

_____ 9. Which of these statements best describes the trading relationship between the United States and Canada?

   A. "You can't change a tiger's stripes."
   B. "No taxation without representation."
   C. "Economics has made us partners."
   D. *Je me souviens*

_____ 10. Why do the United States and Canada continue to attract so many immigrants?

   A. Both are wealthy nations with stable governments.
   B. Both have warm, attractive climates.
   C. Both are countries that have had few immigrants in the past.
   D. Both have huge areas of land that are good for family farmers.

_____ 11. What happened to most of the treaties the United States made with Native American groups?

   A. Most of the treaties ran out after 100 years.
   B. Most of the treaties are still in force.
   C. They were broken so that Native Americans could take European land.
   D. They were broken so that settlers could take Native American land.

_____ 12. How are reservations and reserves alike?

   A. Both are areas set aside by the government for indigenous people.
   B. Both are special government farms for indigenous people.
   C. Both are areas originally owned and inhabited by indigenous people.
   D. Both are areas where European settlers and indigenous people fought battles.

Name _____ Date _____ Class _____

The United States and Canada Practice Test B (continued)

_____ 13. Why are many cities in the Northeast United States located along rivers or near the Atlantic Ocean?
   A. The cities began as recreation areas.
   B. The cities were established within the past 50 years.
   C. The cities began as transportation and trade centers.
   D. The cities grew up near local airports.

_____ 14. What do textile mills make?
   A. They make textbooks.
   B. They grind flour.
   C. They cut lumber for buildings.
   D. They make cloth.

_____ 15. Since 1980, more than one million American farmers have
   A. expanded their farms.
   B. changed from growing wheat to growing soybeans.
   C. stopped working the land.
   D. begun growing crops organically.

_____ 16. What did the United States Congress do to preserve parts of the West?
   A. Congress created national parks and forests.
   B. Congress built dams and hydroelectric plants.
   C. Congress limited the number of new houses that could be built.
   D. Congress planted new trees.

_____ 17. Francophones are people who speak
   A. both French and English.
   B. and read the old Frankish language.
   C. English as their first language.
   D. French as their first language.

_____ 18. How did European settlers affect the lives of the indigenous people in the Canadian prairie?
   A. The indigenous people helped the settlers learn how to respect the land.
   B. European settlers killed most of the buffalo, which were the foundation of life for the indigenous people.
   C. European settlers helped the indigenous people learn how to respect the land.
   D. European settlers built only in areas that the indigenous people had not already claimed.

_____ 19. In the Atlantic provinces, one expanding industry is aquaculture, or
   A. fish farming.
   B. growing wheat in deep pools of water.
   C. growing very small vegetables.
   D. growing vegetables with unusual colors.

© Pearson Education, Inc., publishing as Pearson Prentice Hall. All rights reserved.

The United States and Canada Practice Test B (continued)

_____ 20. Why do the Northwest Territories have such a low population?

    A. The territories are far from Canada's capital.

    B. They are too small to support people.

    C. The territories have very rugged terrain and a harsh climate.

    D. The territories have only recently become part of Canada.

Directions: *Read each question and write your answer on the lines provided.*

21. Why are the Great Lakes important to both the United States and Canada?

_____

_____

_____

_____

22. The United States and Canada both gained independence from Great Britain. How did their methods differ?

_____

_____

_____

_____

23. What is one example of cultural exchange during the settlement of North America?

_____

_____

_____

_____

24. What is one important similarity between the Midwest of the United States and the Prairie Provinces of Canada?

_____

_____

_____

_____

© Pearson Education, Inc., publishing as Pearson Prentice Hall. All rights reserved.

Name _____ Date _____ Class _____

The United States and Canada Practice Test C

Directions: *Read each question and choose the best answer. Then write the letter for the answer you have chosen in each blank.*

_____ 1. How are the Mississippi River in the United States and the Mackenzie River in Canada alike?
   A. Both are important transportation routes.
   B. Both are the longest rivers in their countries.
   C. Both flow from central areas of North America into oceans.
   D. all of the above

_____ 2. What is an important difference between the tundra and grasslands?
   A. Trees grow in the tundra but not in grasslands.
   B. Permanently frozen soil is part of the tundra but not part of grasslands.
   C. Crops grow well in the tundra but not in grasslands.
   D. The tundra is flat, and grasslands are mountainous.

_____ 3. Some scientists think that Native Americans migrated from _____ during the Ice Age.
   A. Europe
   B. Asia
   C. Spain
   D. England

_____ 4. Which statement best explains why the Louisiana Purchase of 1803 was important to the development of the United States?
   A. It created new taxes on imported goods.
   B. It resulted in immigration from France.
   C. It doubled the size of the country.
   D. It encouraged Native Americans to settle more land in the West.

_____ 5. The United States feared the Soviets were trying to expand their power throughout the world. This fear resulted in
   A. World War II.
   B. the Cold War.
   C. World War I.
   D. the fight for civil rights.

_____ 6. What was one important result of the Canadian constitution of 1982?
   A. Quebec became an independent nation.
   B. English became the official language of Canada.
   C. Canada became completely independent.
   D. A monarchy was established in Canada.

© Pearson Education, Inc., publishing as Pearson Prentice Hall. All rights reserved.

The United States and Canada Practice Test C (continued)

_____ 7. Which statement best describes immigration in North America?

    A. Both the United States and Canada have attracted immigrants throughout their histories.

    B. Until about 100 years ago, both the United States and Canada attracted immigrants.

    C. About 100 years ago, both the United States and Canada began to attract immigrants.

    D. Canada now attracts immigrants, but the United States does not.

_____ 8. American literature became more varied as it reflected

    A. the Protestant point of view.

    B. early American authors.

    C. the views of Americans prior to World War I.

    D. the diversity in American culture.

_____ 9. Over the past 50 years, the region of the South in the United States has changed from an agriculture-based economy to

    A. a trade-based economy.

    B. a mining-based economy.

    C. a forest-based economy.

    D. an industry-based economy.

_____ 10. What caused the sudden growth of San Francisco in the middle of the 1800s?

    A. Gold was discovered in the mountains.

    B. The entertainment industry began to grow.

    C. The first national parks were established.

    D. The Civil War was about to begin.

_____ 11. What is one change brought about by the Quiet Revolution in Quebec's government?

    A. The government made English the official language.

    B. The government kept immigrants from living in Quebec.

    C. The government modernized education and health care in Quebec.

    D. The government made Quebec a separate country.

_____ 12. Why are the Canadian Plains called "Canada's Breadbasket"?

    A. The region is a major manufacturing center.

    B. The region is a major wheat-growing center.

    C. The region is a major mining center.

    D. The region is a major shipping center.

© Pearson Education, Inc., publishing as Pearson Prentice Hall. All rights reserved.

Name _____ Date _____ Class _____

The United States and Canada Practice Test C (continued)

Directions: *Read each question and write your answer on the lines provided.*

13. What is the most important difference between the climate of the United States and the climate of Canada? What is the reason for that difference?

   _____
   _____
   _____
   _____

14. What is the difference between the "melting pot" in the United States and the "mosaic of separate pieces" in Canada?

   _____
   _____
   _____
   _____

15. The Macdonald-Cartier Bridge stretches across the Ottawa River and connects Ontario and Quebec. Why is this bridge significant?

   _____
   _____
   _____
   _____

Name _____ Date _____ Class _____

The United States and Canada Practice Test C *(continued)*

16. In a short three-paragraph essay, discuss the meaning of this quotation about the United States and Canada by President John F. Kennedy: "Geography has made us neighbors. History has made us friends. Economics has made us partners."

Name _____ Date _____ Class _____

Africa Study Sheet

Key Terms

apartheid the legal system of treating whites and nonwhites by different rules in South Africa

authoritarian government a nondemocratic form of government in which a single leader or small group of leaders has all the power

bazaar a traditional open-air market with shops or rows of stalls

boycott a refusal to buy or use certain products or services

cash crop a crop that is raised for sale

casbah the older part of a North African city

city-state a city that is also an independent state, with its own traditions, government, and laws

civilization a society that has cities, a government, and social classes and that usually has writing, art, and architecture

clan a group of lineages

colonize to settle in an area and take control of its government

commercial farming the large-scale production of crops for sale

compound a fenced-in group of homes

coup d'état the sudden overthrow of a government by force

cultural diffusion the spread of customs and ideas from one culture to another

cultural diversity a wide variety of cultures

culture the way of life of a people who share similar customs and beliefs

democracy a government in which citizens exercise power through elected representatives

desertification the change of fertile land into land that is too dry or damaged to support life

discriminate to treat people differently, and often unfairly, based on race, religion, or sex

diversify to add variety; expand a country's economy by increasing the variety of goods produced

domesticate to adapt plants or animals and breed them for human use

drought a long period of little or no rain

economy a system for producing, distributing, consuming, and owning goods and services

elevation the height of land above sea level

ethnic group a group of people who share the same ancestors, customs, language, or religion

extended family the part of a family that includes the nuclear family plus other relatives

fellaheen rural farmers in Egypt or other Arab countries

fertile rich in substances that plants need to grow well

Geez an ancient Ethiopian language that was once used to write literature and religious texts but is no longer spoken

harambee a social policy started by Jomo Kenyatta and meaning "let's pull together" in Swahili

Hausa-Fulani Nigeria's largest ethnic group

heritage the values, traditions, and customs handed down from one's ancestors

hybrid a plant that is created by breeding different types of the same plant

Igbo Nigeria's third-largest ethnic group

irrigate to supply with water through a ditch, pipe, channel, or sprinkler

Kikuyu the largest ethnic group in Kenya

kinship a family relationship

life expectancy the average length of time a person can expect to live

lineage group of families that can trace descent back to a common ancestor

Name _____ Date _____ Class _____

lingua-franca a language used for communication among people who speak different languages

literate able to read and write

Maasai a seminomadic ethnic group in Kenya

migrant worker a laborer who travels away from where he or she lives to find work

migrate to move from one place to settle in another

monastery a place where people, especially men known as monks, live a religious life

multiethnic having many ethnic groups living within a society

multiparty system a political system in which two or more parties compete in elections

nationalism a feeling of pride for one's homeland; a group's identity as members of a nation

nationalize to transfer ownership of something to a nation's government

nomad a person who has no permanent settled home and who instead moves from place to place

nuclear family the part of a family that includes parents and children

oasis a fertile place in a desert where there is water and vegetation

overgrazing allowing too much grazing by large herds of animals

Pan-Africanism the belief that Africans should work together for their rights and freedoms

pilgrimage a religious journey

plantation a large farm where cash crops are grown

plateau a large, level area that rises above the surrounding land

privatization the sale of government-owned industries to private companies

Quran the sacred book of Islam

rift a deep trench or crack in Earth's surface

savanna a region of tall grasses with scattered trees

Sharia Islamic law, based on the words and deeds of Muhammad and on comments written by Muslim scholars and lawmakers

souq an open-air marketplace in an Arab city

sovereignty independence; a country having political control over itself

subsistence farming raising just enough crops to support one's family

Swahili aBantu language, that contains some Arab words, spoken in much of East Africa

terrace a flat platform cut into the side of a slope, used for growing crops

Yoruba Nigeria's second-largest ethnic group

Key Places

Aksum a bustling trade center along the Red Sea; ancient kingdom of East Africa, in what is now Ethiopia and Eritrea

Aswan High Dam built by Egypt's government to control flooding of the Nile; created Lake Nasser; source of hydroelectricity

Cairo the capital of Egypt and the most populous city in Africa

Cape Town former Dutch colony in South Africa; once the home of Afrikaners

Congo, Democratic Republic of the Africa's third largest country; located in west Central Africa; formerly Zaire

Congo River a river that flows through the rain forest of the country of Congo in Central Africa; 2,900 miles (4,677 km) long, Africa's second-longest river

Egypt an ancient civilization of the Nile Valley ruled by pharaohs; advanced in paper making, architecture, medicine, and mathematics

Ghana ancient trade empire located between the Senegal and Niger rivers; succeeded by the kingdom of Mali; British West African colony of the Gold Coast, achieved independence in 1957

© Pearson Education, Inc., publishing as Pearson Prentice Hall. All rights reserved.

Great Rift Valley a deep trench in Africa formed millions of years ago, when the continents pulled apart

Kenya country in central East Africa

Mali, Kingdom of arose in the mid-1200s in the Upper Niger Valley

Mount Kenya Kenya's highest mountain, located just south of the Equator

Mount Kilimanjaro the highest mountain in Africa; located in northeastern Tanzania

Niger River Africa's third-longest river, which begins in the West African country of Guinea

Nile River longest river in the world; sources are the White Nile in Sudan and the Blue Nile in Ethiopia; flows into the Mediterranean

Nile Valley land surrounding the Nile River; farmed for thousands of years

Nubia an ancient kingdom south of Egypt

Sahara the world's largest desert

Sahel region where the southern edge of the Sahara meets the savanna

Songhai powerful West African kingdom; controlled important trade routes and wealthy trading centers

South Africa, Republic of a country ruled until the 1990s by a minority group of white people who instituted apartheid; richest and most industrialized country on the continent of Africa

Tombouctou the wealthiest Songhai trading city, located along the Niger River

Zambezi River a river of Southern Africa that runs through or forms the borders of six countries: Angola, Zambia, Namibia, Botswana, Zimbabwe, and Mozambique

Key People

de Klerk, F.W. South Africa's president in 1990, who helped to pass laws that ended apartheid

Equiano, Olaudah a former slave who bought his own freedom and became an antislavery activist; wrote an account of his enslavement

Kenyatta, Jomo first president of Kenya

Leakey, Louis archaeologist who found some of the first evidence of early people in East Africa

Mandela, Nelson African National Congress (ANC) president jailed for almost 30 years; South Africa's first president after apartheid ended in the 1990s

Mansa Musa Mali's most famous king; made a pilgrimage to Mecca in 1324, building new trading ties with other Muslim states

Nkrumah, Kwame leader who organized protest against British rule in the early 1950s; became Ghana's first president in 1960

Rawlings, Jerry president of Ghana in the 1980s who tried to reform the country's politics and economy; stressed the traditional African values of hard work and sacrifice

Seko, Mobutu Sese military leader of the Congo who renamed the country Zaire and ruled with authoritarian power from the 1960s to the 1990s, when he was exiled

Senghor, Leopold Sedar one of the greatest Pan-African leaders, a poet and political leader who encouraged Africans to study their traditions and to be proud of their culture; became Senegal's first president in 1960

The Ancient World Study Sheet

Key Terms

absolute power complete control over someone or something

ahimsa in Hinduism, the idea of being nonviolent

caravan a group traveling together

caste a social class of people

citadel a fortress in a city

city-state a city that is also a separate independent state

civil service the group of people whose job it is to carry out the work of the government

civilization a society with cities, a central government run by official leaders, and workers who specialize in various jobs, and social classes

code an organized list of laws or rules

covenant a promise made by God

culture language, religious beliefs, values, customs, and other ways of life shared by a group of people

cuneiform form of writing that uses groups of wedges and lines; used to write several languages of the Fertile Crescent

dharma the religious and moral duties of Hindus

diaspora the scattering of people who have a common background or beliefs

dictator a ruler who has total control of the government

disciple a follower of a person or belief

dynasty a series of rulers from the same family

empire many territories and people who are controlled by one government

extended family closely related people of several generations

hieroglyphs pictures and other written symbols that stand for ideas, things, or sounds

Hinduism a religion developed in India, introduced by the Aryans, and based on sacred books called the Vedas and Upanishads; many gods recognized as different aspects of one supreme being

inflation an economic situation in which there is more money with less value

Islam the religion practiced by Muslims; based on the teachings of the prophet Muhammad and on the holy book of Islam, the Quran

Judaism the religion of the Jewish people which developed from ancient Israelite beliefs; based on belief in one God and the teachings of the sacred texts, the Hebrew Bible

merchant a person who buys or sells goods for a profit; person who runs a store or business

Middle Kingdom the period from about 1991 to 1786 B.C., during which Dynasty 12 ruled ancient Egypt; a name for the land of ancient China

missionary a person who spreads his or her religious beliefs to others

monotheism the belief in one god

monsoon a strong, seasonal wind that blows across a region

moral acting in a way that is considered good and just by a society's standards

mummy a dead body preserved in a lifelike condition

myth a traditional story; in some cultures, a legend that explains people's beliefs

New Kingdom the period from about 1567 to 1085 B.C., during which dynasties 18, 19, and 20 ruled ancient Egypt

New Stone Age the later part of the Stone Age during which people began to grow their own foods and lived in the same place year after year

nirvana the lasting peace that Buddhists seek by giving up selfish desires

noble in certain societies, a person of high rank; in early civilizations, members of the upper class who were government officials

nomad a person who has no single, settled home

Old Kingdom the period from about 2686 to 2181 B.C., during which dynasties 3, 4, and 5 ruled ancient Egypt

Name _____ Date _____ Class _____

Old Stone Age the early part of the Stone Age during which people learned to hunt in groups, discovered how to use fire, and became nomads

papyrus an early form of paper made from a reedlike plant found in the marshy areas of the Nile Delta

patrician member of a wealthy, upper-class family in the Roman Republic

peasant member of a class that makes its living through small-scale farming and labor

pharaoh a king of ancient Egypt

philosopher someone who uses reason to understand the world; in Greece, the earliest philosophers used reason to explain natural events

plebeian an ordinary citizen in the ancient Roman Republic

polytheism the belief in many gods

prophet a teacher who is regarded as speaking for God or a god

reincarnation the rebirth of the soul in the body of another living thing

republic a type of government in which citizens who have the right to vote select their leaders

Roman Empire an empire lasting from 27 B.C. to A.D. 476, whose boundaries changed over time but at their greatest length stretched from Britain to North Africa and the Persian Gulf

Rosetta Stone an ancient tablet covered with Egyptian and Greek hieroglyphics; provided a key to deciphering hieroglyphics

society a group of people, distinct from other groups, who share a common culture

Stone Age a period of time during which people made lasting tools and weapons mainly from stone; the earliest known period of human culture

Torah the most sacred text of the early Israelites; recorded their laws and history

Upanishads one of the Hindu religious texts; written in the style of questions by students and answers by teachers

ziggurat a temple of the ancient Sumerians and Babylonians, made of terraces connected by ramps and stairs, roughly in the shape of a pyramid

Key Places

Place	Description
Arabian Peninsula	a peninsula of Southwest Asia
Asia	the world's largest continent
Asia Minor	a peninsula in western Asia
Assyria	a historical kingdom of northern Mesopotamia
Athens	a city-state of ancient Greece
Babylonia	an ancient region around southeastern Mesopotamia, lying between the Tigris and Euphrates Rivers
Byzantium	a city of ancient Greece
Cairo	the capital and largest city of Egypt, located on the Nile River
Dead Sea	a salt lake between Israel and Jordan; the lowest point on Earth
Euphrates River	a river flowing south from Turkey through Syria and Iraq
Fertile Crescent	a region in Southwest Asia; site of the world's first civilizations
Ganges River	a river in northern India and Bangladesh, flowing from the Himalaya Mountains to the Bay of Bengal

© Pearson Education, Inc., publishing as Pearson Prentice Hall. All rights reserved.

	Himalaya Mountains	a mountain system of south central Asia, that extends along the border between India and Tibet and through Pakistan, Nepal, and Bhutan
	Hindu Kush	a mountain range in central Asia
	Indus River	a river that rises in Tibet, crosses the Himalaya Mountains, and flows through India and Pakistan into the Arabian Sea. Its valley was the home to India's earliest communities.
	Lower Egypt	an area in ancient Egypt in the northern Nile River region
	Lower Nubia	an ancient region in northern Africa extending from the Nile Valley in Egypt to present-day Sudan, specifically, between the first and second Nile cataracts
	Macedonia	an ancient kingdom of the Balkan Peninsula in southeastern Europe
	Maurya Empire	the Indian empire founded by Chandragupta; began with his kingdom in northeastern India and spread to most of northern and central India
	Mesopotamia	an ancient region between the Tigris and Euphrates rivers in Southwest Asia
	Napata	one of the three most powerful Nubian kingdoms; located between the third and fourth cataracts of the Nile River in Upper Nubia
	New Babylonian Empire	a revival of the old Babylonian empire stretching from the Persian Gulf to the Mediterranean Sea
	Nile River	the longest river in the world, flowing through northeastern Africa into the Mediterranean Sea
	North China Plain	a large plain in East Asia, built up by soil deposits of the Huang River
	Nubia	a desert region and ancient kingdom in the Nile River Valley
	Persia	a vast ancient empire of Southwest Asia
	Persian Gulf	an arm of the Arabian Sea, located between the Arabian Peninsula and southwest Iran
	Phoenicia	an ancient region in present-day Lebanon
	Rome	capital of the ancient Roman Empire
	Sahara	the largest desert in the world; covers almost all of North Africa
	Silk Road	an ancient trade route between China and Europe
	Sparta	an ancient city-state in Greece
	Sumer	the site of the earliest known civilization; located in Mesopotamia, later became Babylonia
	Tiber River	a major river in Italy; flows through Rome
	Tigris River	a river in Iraq and Turkey
	Tyre	a rich trade port and the major city of Phoenicia
	Upper Egypt	an area of ancient Egypt in the Nile Valley, south of the river's delta
	Upper Nubia	an ancient region in northeastern Africa that extended from the Nile Valley in Egypt to present-day Sudan, specifically between the second and sixth cataracts
	Ur	a city of ancient Sumer in southern Mesopotamia

© Pearson Education, Inc., publishing as Pearson Prentice Hall. All rights reserved.

Name _____ Date _____ Class _____

Asia and the Pacific Study Sheet

Key Terms

alluvial made of soil deposited by rivers

aquaculture fish farming

arable land land that can produce crops

archipelago a group of islands

atoll a small coral island in the shape of a ring

birthrate the number of live births each year per 1,000 people

boycott a refusal to buy or use goods and services, to show disapproval or to bring about change

cash crop a crop that is raised to be sold for money on the world market

caste in the Hindu religion, a social group in which people are born and which they cannot change; each group with assigned jobs

civil war a war between political parties or regions within the same country

clan a group of families with a common ancestor

collective farm in a communist country, a large farm formed from many private farms collected into a single unit by the government

colony a territory ruled by another nation

commune a community in which people own land as a group and where they live and work together

communist relating to a government that controls a country's industries, businesses, and land

copra dried coconut meat

coral a rocklike material made up of the skeletons of tiny sea creatures

cultural diffusion the spreading of ideas or practices from one culture to another

deciduous falling off or shedding, as in leaves

demilitarized zone an area in which no weapons are allowed; DMZ

desert a dry region that has extreme temperatures and little vegetation

developing country a country that has low industrial production and little modern technology

developed country a country with many industries and a well-developed economy

dialect variation of a language that is unique to a region or an area

dictatorship a form of government in which power is held by a leader who has absolute authority

diversify to add variety

domino theory a belief that if one country fell to communism, neighboring countries would also fall

double-cropping growing two or more crops on the same land

dynasty a series of rulers from the same family

emperor a male ruler of an empire

ethnic group people who share such characteristics as language, religion, and ancestry

famine a huge food shortage

fertile able to support plant growth

fiord a long narrow inlet or arm of the sea bordered by steep slopes created by glaciers

free enterprise an economic system in which people can choose their own jobs, start private businesses, own property, and make a profit

geyser a hot spring that shoots a jet of water and steam into the air

glacier a huge, slow-moving mass of snow and ice

green revolution a worldwide effort to increase food production in developing countries

gross domestic product the total value of all goods and services produced in an economy

hajj pilgrimage to Mecca undertaken by Muslims

high island a island formed by the mountainous top of an ancient volcano

© Pearson Education, Inc., publishing as Pearson Prentice Hall. All rights reserved.

Name _____ Date _____ Class _____

Hinduism major world religion; belief that various gods and goddesses represent one spirit

Holocaust the systematic killing of more than six million European Jews and others by Nazi Germany before and during World War II

homogenous identical or similar

incentive benefit offered

isolationism separateness

Khmer Empire an empire that included much of present-day Cambodia, Thailand, Malaysia, and parts of Laos

Khmer Rouge the Cambodian Communist party

kibbutz a cooperative settlement

landlocked having no direct access to the sea

life expectancy the average number of years a person can be expected to live

low island an island formed from coral reefs or atolls

marsupial an animal such as a kangaroo that carries its young in a body pouch

monarchy a state or nation in which power is held by a monarch—a king, queen, or an emperor

monotheism a belief that there is only one god

monsoon a wind that changes direction with the change of season

muezzin a person whose job it is to call Muslims to pray

nationalist a person devoted to the interests of his or her country

nomad a person who has no settled home but who moves from place to place

nonrenewable resource a resource that cannot quickly be replaced once it is used

paddy a level field that is flooded to grow rice

partition division into parts or portions

penal colony a place settled by convicts, or prisoners

plain a large area of flat or gently rolling land

plateau a raised area of level land bordered on one or more sides by steep slopes or cliffs

population density average number of people living in a square mile (or square km)

Quran the holy book of Islam

radical extreme

recession a period of time in which an economy and the businesses that support it shrink

Red Guard groups of Chinese who carried out Mao Zedong's policies

refugee a person who flees from his or her country because of war

self-sufficient able to supply one's needs without any assistance

standard of living a measurement of a person's or a group's education, housing, health, and nutrition

station in Australia, a large ranch

strait a narrow stretch of water that connects two larger bodies of water

subcontinent a large landmass that is a major part of a continent

subsidy to support financially

subsistence farming farming that provides only enough food for a family or a village

tectonic plate a huge slab of rock that moves very slowly over a softer layer beneath the surface of Earth's crust

terrace a level area in a hillside

tourism the business of providing services for tourists

Key Places

Adelaide the capital of South Australia, on the southern coast of Australia

Alice Springs a town in Northern Territory, Australia

Angkor Wat the largest temple in the world; a Hindu temple deep in the rain forests of Cambodia built in the A.D. 1100s by the Khmer

Auckland the largest city in New Zealand, located on North Island

Australia Earth's largest island and smallest continent; also the name of the sole country that exists on this continent

Brunei a small kingdom on the northwestern coast of the island of Borneo; an Islamic nation with large deposits of oil and the largest palace in the world

Canberra the national capital of Australia, in southeastern Australia

Canterbury Plain flat, fertile land on New Zealand's South Island

Caroline Islands Micronesian islands in the central Pacific Ocean

Chang Chinese river that flows to the East China Sea and is the only river in East Asia deep enough for cargo ships to sail on

Coral Sea an arm of the Pacific Ocean, located between Australia and the Solomon Islands

Darling River a major river in eastern Australia

Easter Island an island in the eastern Pacific Ocean, part of Polynesia; known for its giant human head statues

Euphrates River river of western Asia; combines with the Tigris River in Iraq; site of ancient civilizations

Fiji a large Pacific island

French Polynesia a country in the south Pacific Ocean roughly midway between Australia and South America; part of Polynesia

Ganges River river that flows in a wide sweeping arc across northern India

Gilbert Islands Micronesian islands in the central Pacific Ocean

Great Barrier Reef the long series of coral reefs running along the northeastern coast of Australia; about 1,250 miles (2,010km) in length

Great Dividing Range mountains just to the west of the coastal plain in Australia

Great Sandy Desert a desert in western Australia

Guam Micronesian island, located in the Northern Mariana Islands in the central Pacific Ocean, administered by the United States

Hawaii the fiftieth state of the United States; island group in the central Pacific Ocean; part of Polynesia

Himalaya Mountains a mountain range that contains the world's tallest peaks

Huang River Chinese river that runs through a fertile region called the North China Plain; known as Yellow River

Indus River river that flows westward from the Himalayas into the country of Pakistan

Kashmir a land of high mountains and beautiful lakes, and the source of the Indus River; site of an ongoing struggle between Pakistan and India

Kiribati Polynesian island nation in the south Pacific Ocean

Lake Eyre salt lake located in south, central Australia; world's largest internally draining area

Mariana Islands Micronesian islands in the central Pacific Ocean

Marshall Islands Micronesian island nation in the central Pacific Ocean

Mauna Kea volcanic peak in Hawaii

Melbourne the capital of Victoria; Australia's second largest city; located on the southern coast of Australia

Melanesia island region north and east of Australia; "black islands"

Mesopotamia the region along the Tigris and Euphrates Rivers, an ancient center of farming and trade

Name _____ Date _____ Class _____

Micronesia island region north of the Equator, covering an area as large as the continental United States; "small islands"

Midway Islands two islands, Eastern and Sand, in the central Pacific Ocean, administered by the United States; part of Polynesia

Mount Cook highest peak in New Zealand's Southern Alps; located on South Island

Mount Everest world's tallest mountain; located in the Himalaya Mountains

Murray River a major river of Australia

Nauru Polynesian island nation in the south Pacific Ocean

Negev Desert the lowest point on Earth; makes up the southern two thirds of the country of Israel

New Caledonia Melanesian island nation in the south Pacific Ocean

New Zealand country made up of North Island and South Island; formed by volcanoes

North China Plain huge area around the Huang River; one of the best farming areas in China

North Island the smaller and more northern of the two islands composing New Zealand

outback desert and dry grassland; the huge central plain of Australia

Pacific Rim nations that border the Pacific Ocean involved in trade; includes Australia, New Zealand, Japan, South Korea, China, Hong Kong, Taiwan, and the United States; Australia's economy depends on trade with these countries

Palestine an area along the eastern shore of the Mediterranean Sea; an area of dispute between Jews and Arabs

Papua New Guinea the largest and most populated Melanesian country

Pitcairn Island Polynesian island in the central Pacific Ocean, administered by the United Kingdom

Polynesia the largest island region in the Pacific, including Hawaii, Tahiti, and Samoa; "many islands"

Samoa nation made up of many islands in the south Pacific Ocean; part of Polynesia

Solomon Islands a nation of islands in the South Pacific; part of Melanesia

South Island the larger and more southern of the two islands composing New Zealand

Southern Alps mountain range on New Zealand's South Island

Sydney the capital of New South Wales; on the southeastern coast of Australia

Tahiti a Pacific island; a very popular tourist destination; part of Polynesia

Taiwan an island off China's southeast coast

Taj Mahal monument Shah Jahan built to honor his deceased wife

Tasmania island located off the southeastern coast of Australia

Tigris River river of western Asia that combines with the Euphrates River in Iraq; site of ancient civilizations

Tonga nation made up of many islands in the south Pacific Ocean; part of Polynesia

Tuamotus Polynesian islands in the central Pacific Ocean

Tuvalu island nation in the south Pacific Ocean; part of Polynesia, Melanesia, and Micronesia

Uluru landmark monolith in Australia's outback; formerly known as Ayers Rock

Vanuatu a nation made up of many islands in the Pacific Ocean; part of Melanesia

Wellington the capital of New Zealand, located on North Island

West Bank a disputed region on the western bank of the Jordan River

Western Samoa Polynesian island nation in the South Pacific

Name _____ Date _____ Class _____

Key People

Aborigines a member of the earliest people of Australia, who probably came from Asia

Abraham believed to be the originator of Judaism; lived in Mesopotamia over 3,000 years ago

Asoka ruler of the Maurya empire who spread the peaceful message of Buddhism throughout his empire

Confucius philosopher in ancient China

Cook, James British sea captain; explored New Zealand and Australia; claimed both lands for Britain

Dalai Lama, the spiritual and temporal ruler of Tibet; has ruled in exile since 1959 and pursues a nonviolent campaign to end Chinese occupation of Tibet

Gandhi, Mohandas K. leader who urged Indians to resist the British by following Hindu traditions, particularly nonviolence

Hammurabi ruler of Babylon from 1800 B.C. to 1750 B.C.; author of Hammurabi's Code, laws that governed ancient Babylonians

Hillary, Sir Edmund New Zealander, who along with Tenzing Norgay of Nepal, was the first to reach the summit of Mount Everest

Ho Chi Minh Vietnamese independence leader and communist ruler of North Vietnam

Jesus believed by Christians to be Christ or the messiah; accounts of whose life form an important part of the New Testament in the Christian Bible

Maori a native of New Zealand whose ancestors first traveled from Asia to Polynesia, and later to New Zealand

Muhammad the prophet of Islam whose teachings form the basis of Islam's holy book, the Quran

Siddhartha Gautama also known as the Buddha, or "Enlightened One," founder of Buddhism

Zedong, Mao Chinese communist leader; known for Great Leap Forward and Cultural Revolution

Name_____ Date_____ Class_____

Major Industries in Australia, New Zealand, and the Pacific Island Nations

Nation	Major Industries
Australia	mining, industrial and transportation equipment, food processing, chemical, steel, textiles and clothing, metal products, tourism
New Zealand	food processing, wood and paper products, textiles and clothing, machinery, transportation equipment, banking and insurance, tourism, mining, petroleum refining, chemicals, metal products
Federated States of Micronesia	tourism, construction, fish processing, craft items
Fiji	food processing, tourism, mining, clothing, lumbering, small cottage industries
Kiribati	coconut processing, craft items
Marshall Islands	coconut processing, tourism, craft items
Nauru	mining, financial services; coconut processing
Palau	tourism, craft items
Papua New Guinea	food processing, plywood and wood chips, mining, petroleum, construction, tourism
Samoa	tourism, food processing, lumbering, motor vehicle parts
Solomon Islands	food processing, mining
Tonga	tourism, construction
Tuvalu	tourism, coconut processing
Vanuatu	food processing, wood processing, tourism, off-shore banking

Major Dynasties of China

Dynasty	Time Period	Important Events and Cultural Contributions
Shang	1766 B.C.- 1122 B.C.	• Well-developed writing • First Chinese calendar, bronze casting
Zhou	1122 B.C. – 256 B.C.	• Writing laws • Iron tools and plows in use
Qin	211 B.C. – 206 B.C.	• First great Chinese empire • Much of Great Wall built • Introduced standard weights and measures
Han	206 B.C. – A.D. 220	• Chinese trace their ancestry to this dynasty • Paper, compass, seismograph invented • Buddhism introduced • Government based on Confucianism
Tang	A.D. 618 – A.D. 907	• Sculpture and poetry flourish

© Pearson Education, Inc., publishing as Pearson Prentice Hall. All rights reserved.

Dynasty	Time Period	Important Events and Cultural Contributions
Song	A.D. 960 – A.D. 1279	• Block printing and paper money developed • Gunpowder first used
Ming	A.D. 1368 – A.D. 1644	• Artists and philosophers make China a highly civilized country • Porcelain, the novel, and drama flourish
Qing	A.D. 1644 – A.D. 1911	• Increased trade with Europe • Last dynasty ends with Emperor Pu Yi

Events in Japanese History

Year	Event
300 B.C.	Japanese learn irrigated rice cultivation and metalworking from Asian continent.
A.D. 405	Japan accepts the use of Chinese characters to write Japanese.
A.D. 1000	A woman writes the world's first novel, *The Tale of Genji*.
A.D. 1543	Portuguese traders introduce guns and Christianity.
A.D. 1640	Japan closes its borders to the rest of the world.
A.D. 1853	Commodore Perry and American warships arrive in Japan, Japanese then agree to trade with the United States and other nations.

© Pearson Education, Inc., publishing as Pearson Prentice Hall. All rights reserved.

Name _____ Date _____ Class _____

Europe and Russia Study Sheet

Key Terms

alliance an agreement between countries to protect and defend each other

annex add or attach a new territory to an existing country

capitalism an economic system in which businesses are privately owned

Cold War a period of tension without actual warfare, notably the decades after World War II

colony a territory ruled by another nation

communism a political system in which a country's property and resources belong equally to everyone

constitution a set of laws that describes how a government works

constitutional monarchy a government in which the monarch serves as head of state, but has limited powers

democracy a government in which citizens govern themselves

dialect a version of a language found only in a certain region

dictator a leader with unlimited power

Duma a Russian congress whose members were elected by the people

economic sanctions actions to limit trade with nations that have violated international law

emigrate to move from one country to another

embargo a ban on trade

empire a collection of lands ruled by a single government

entrepreneur a person who develops original ideas in order to start new businesses

ethnic group a group of people who share the same ancestors, culture, language, or religion

euro the official currency of the European Union

famine severe lack of food

feudalism a system in which people had obligations based on their position in society

Flemish Dutch

foreign minister a government official who is in charge of a nation's foreign affairs

free enterprise a system in which businesses can compete with one another for profit, with little government control

genocide the deliberate murder of a racial, political, or ethnic group

heritage the customs and practices passed from one generation to the next

Holocaust the mass murder of six million Jews

humanism a new approach to knowledge that focused on improving the world rather than hoping for a better life after death

hydroelectric power power generated by water-driven turbines

immigrant a person who moves to one country from another

imperialism the political and economic control of one country by another

Industrial Revolution a life-changing period in the 1800s when products began to be made by machines in factories

inflation an increase in the general level of prices

investor someone who spends money on improving a business in the hope of making more money

land reform the process of dividing large properties into smaller ones

loess a type of rich, dust-like soil

manufacturing the process of turning raw materials into finished products

Middle Ages the time between ancient and modern times, about A.D. 500-1500

migration movement from place to place

monarch the ruler of a kingdom or empire, such as a king or queen

multicultural related to many different cultures

nationalism pride in one's country

national debt the amount of money a government owes

© Pearson Education, Inc., publishing as Pearson Prentice Hall. All rights reserved.

Name _____ Date _____ Class _____

navigable wide and deep enough for ships to travel through

nonrenewable resources resources that cannot be replenished after they are used

Parliament the lawmaking body of the United Kingdom

Pax Romana 200 years of peace under the Roman Empire

peninsula land area nearly surrounded by water

permafrost a permanently frozen layer of ground below the top layer of soil

persecution harassment

philosophy a system of ideas and beliefs

plateau a large raised area of mostly level land bordered on one or more sides by steep slopes or cliffs

polder patch of land reclaimed from below sea level

population density the average number of people living in a square mile or a square kilometer

prairie grassland

privatization the return of businesses from government to private ownership and management

propaganda the spread of ideas designed to support a cause or hurt an opposing cause

Renaissance a period of European history that included the rebirth of interest in learning and art

representative a person who represents, or speaks for, a group of people

repress to put down

reunification the process of becoming unified again

revolution a far-reaching change

revolutionary ideas that relate to or cause the overthrow of a government, or other great changes

secede to leave a group, especially a political group or nation

serf a peasant who could not leave the land of a lord for whom he or she worked in exchange for protection

Scientific Revolution time during which scientists began to base theories on facts by watching carefully to see what really happened in the world

single market a system in which goods, services, and capital move freely, with no barrier

standard of living the level of comfort in terms of the goods and services that people have

steppes the grasslands of fertile soil suitable for farming in Russia

tariff a fee charged by a government on goods entering the country

textile a cloth product

tributary a smaller river or stream that feeds into a larger river

tsar a Russian emperor

tundra a cold, dry, treeless region covered with snow for most of the year

United Nations a group of countries that works together to bring about peace and cooperation among the nations of the world

urbanization the movement of populations toward cities

welfare state a country in which many services and benefits are paid for by the government

westernization the adoption of western European culture

Key Places

Balkans a region located south of the Danube River made up of several countries, populated primarily by Christian Orthodox, Roman Catholics, and Muslims

Bosnia-Herzegovina battleground for bitter struggle among Serbians, Croatians, and Bosnian Muslims

Czech Republic formerly part of Czechoslovakia; predominantly Czech population

Eurasia the world's largest landmass

Europe a continent made up of 47 different countries and four major land regions

Greece center of ancient language, culture, and ideas spread by Alexander the Great throughout the Mediterranean

Northern Ireland Protestant part of Ireland that has political and economic ties to Great Britain

North Sea body of water rich in oil and gas deposits

Norway Scandinavian nation where people must contend with a very short growing season; relies on water for almost all of its electric power

Ruhr Valley rich coal-mining region of Germany

Russia the largest country in the world; has one third of the world's coal reserves as well as great reserves of iron ore

Siberia Russian region beyond the Ural Mountains that extends for thousands of miles; rich in oil and gas deposits

Silesia industrial center where Poland, the Czech Republic, and Germany come together; rich in coal

Slovakia homeland of the Slavic peoples, who today are one of the major ethnic groups in Eastern Europe; formerly part of Czechoslovakia

taiga Russian forested region that covers more than 4 million square miles (6.4 million sq km)

Ukraine European region rich in coal

Ural Mountains mountains that mark the boundary between Europe and Asia

Vatican, the an independent city-state located within Rome, led by the Pope; world headquarters of the Roman Catholic Church

Key People

Alexander the Great king of Macedonia who conquered an empire that spread eastward to the Indus River

Aristotle Greek philosopher, teacher of Alexander the Great, known for his observations about the natural world

Catherine the Great a German princess who came to Russia as a young bride of 16 and then seized control of the throne with the support of the people, the military, and the church; opened her court to the teachers, thinkers, and scientists of Western Europe

Elizabeth II current Queen of the United Kingdom, a symbol of Britain's past and its customs

Gorbachev, Mikhail Soviet president who granted the people more personal freedom and loosened economic controls

Henry VIII English king who broke with the Roman Catholic Church in 1541 to form the Protestant Church of England with himself as its head

Hitler, Adolf leader of the Nazi party and German dictator during World War II

Ivan the Terrible Ivan IV, the first Russian czar, crowned in 1547; conquered western Siberia and the Mongol lands to the southeast; known for his cruelty

Jesus of Nazareth founder of Christianity; believed by Christians to be Christ or the messiah; executed by the Roman government

John English king who was forced to sign the Magna Carta in 1215

John Paul II Roman Catholic Pope, a Polish citizen made head of the Church in 1978

Lenin, Vladimir leader who took over the Russian government in 1917 and set up a new communist regime

Louis XIV monarch of France from 1643 to 1715 who believed that his power to rule came from God

Marco Polo explorer who traveled from Venice to the East in the thirteenth century and brought back marvelous tales of the voyage

Tchaikovsky, Peter Russian classical composer

Tolstoy, Leo novelist who wrote powerful stories of life in Russia in the 1800s

Name _____ Date _____ Class _____

Foundations of Geography Study Sheet

Key Terms

absolute location the exact location of a place on Earth

acculturation the process of accepting new ideas and fitting them into a culture

atmosphere the thick layer of gases surrounding Earth

axis an imaginary line running through the center of Earth between the North and South Poles

biodiversity a large variety of living things in a region

birthrate the number of live births each year per 1,000 people

canopy the layer formed by the uppermost branches of a rain forest

civil engineering technology for building structures that alter the landscape, such as dams, roads, and bridges

civilization an advanced culture with cities and the use of writing

climate the average weather conditions of a place over many years

colonization the movement of settlers and their culture to a new country

compass rose a diagram of a compass

constitution a set of laws that defines and often limits the power of government

consumer a person who buys goods and uses services

crust thin layer of rocks and minerals that surrounds the Earth's mantle

cultural diffusion the movement of customs and ideas

cultural landscape the parts of a people's environment that they have shaped and that reflect their culture

cultural traits a particular group's distinct skills, customs, and ways of doing things that form a culture

culture the way of life of a group of people who share similar beliefs and customs

death rate the number of deaths each year per 1,000 people

deforestation a loss of forest cover in a region

demography science that studies the change and distribution of populations

dependency a region that belongs to another state

desert scrub desert vegetation that needs little water

developed nations nations with many industries and advanced technology

developing nations nations with few industries and simple technology

distortion loss of accuracy

economy a system for producing, distributing, and consuming goods and services of value

empire a state containing several countries

Equator the line of latitude around the middle of the globe

erosion a process by which water, wind, or ice wears away landforms and carries material to another place

ethics standards of accepted behavior

fault crack in Earth's crust where plates meet; location of earthquakes

first-level activity the part of the economy that produces raw materials

fossil fuel a source of energy formed over millions of years from animal and plant remains; products include coal, petroleum and natural gas

geography the study of Earth

goods products made for sale or trade

government the system that sets up and enforces a society's laws and institutions

Green Revolution scientific developments in agriculture that have increased the world's food supply

grid evenly spaced intersecting lines used to locate points on a map

hemisphere one half of the Earth, which is divided into northern and southern sections by the Equator

high latitudes the areas north of the Arctic Circle and south of the Antarctic Circle; the polar zone

© Pearson Education, Inc., publishing as Pearson Prentice Hall. All rights reserved.

Name _____ Date _____ Class _____

immigrant a person who leaves one country and moves to another
industrialization the growth of machine-powered production in an economy
key a guide or legend on a map that explains map symbols and shading
landform shape and type of land
latitude imaginary lines that circle the globe from east to west
life expectancy the average number of years that people live
longitude imaginary lines that circle the globe from north to south
low latitudes the area between the Tropic of Cancer and the Tropic of Capricorn; the tropics
mantle the section of Earth just below the crust
magma soft, nearly molten rock
meridian line of longitude
middle latitudes the temperate zones of the Northern and Southern Hemispheres; have seasons
migration the movement of people from one place to another
nation-state a state that is independent of other states
natural resource any useful material found in the environment that can be used for food, clothing, or shelter
nonrenewable resource a resource that cannot be replaced after it is used
orbit the oval-shaped path the Earth makes around the sun
parallel line of latitude
plate piece of Earth's crust that moves over time
plate tectonics theory that Earth's crust is made of huge, slow-moving slabs of rock
population number of people in an area
population density the average number of people per square mile or square kilometer
population distribution description of how population is spread out over an area
precipitation water that falls to the ground as rain, sleet, hail, or snow
Prime Meridian line of 0° longitude that runs through Greenwich, England

producer an owner or worker who makes products
projection method of putting a map of Earth onto a flat piece of paper
push-pull theory a theory of migration that states people migrate because difficulties "push" them to leave while hope of a better life "pulls" them to a new country
raw material natural resource that must be processed to be useful
recyclable resource a resource that recycles through our environment naturally
relative location the location of a place explained by a description of the places near it
renewable resource a natural resource that can be replaced
revolution a full orbit around the sun
rotation each complete turn of Earth, which takes approximately 24 hours
rural located in the countryside
second-level activity manufacturing business; takes materials from primary industries and other secondary industries and makes them into goods
service a function performed by a producer for a consumer
society a group of people sharing a culture
social class a grouping of people based on rank or status
social structure a pattern of organized relationships among groups of people within a society
third-level activity service companies
tundra an area of cold climate and low-lying vegetation
urbanization the movement of people to cities and the resulting growth of cities
vegetation the plants that grow in a particular place
weather day-to-day changes in the air, measured primarily by temperature and precipitation
weathering a process that breaks rocks down into tiny pieces; caused by wind, rain, and ice

© Pearson Education, Inc., publishing as Pearson Prentice Hall. All rights reserved.

Name _____ Date _____ Class _____

Key Economies

Term	Description
capitalism	an economy where private individuals or groups of people own most businesses; motivated by profit
command economy	an economy in which decisions are made by the central government
communist system	an economic system in which the central government owns all property, such as farms and factories, for the benefit of its citizens, controlling all aspects of citizens' lives
free enterprise	an economy that allows private companies to trade and make a profit without government control
market economy	an economy with most businesses privately owned, where prices and wages are determined by the supply and demand of goods
socialist system	an economy in which the government owns most basic industries and runs them for the good of society, not for profit
traditional economy	an economy in which producing, buying, and selling goods operates by the customs, traditions, and habits of the group

Key Governments

Term	Description
dictatorship	a form of government in which one person, the dictator, holds almost total power over its people
direct democracy	a government in which everyone participates in running the affairs of the group
monarchy	a government ruled by a king or queen who inherits the throne by birth
representative democracy	a form of government in which the people indirectly hold the power to rule, electing representatives who create laws

Key Climates

Term	Description
tropical	found in the low latitudes; hot, wet, and sunny; tropical rain forest
dry	little rain and sandy, gravelly soil, sparse vegetation
moderate	found in the middle latitudes; moderate rainfall and temperature; varied vegetation
continental	moderate to hot temperature in the summer; cold in the winter, vegetation includes grasslands and forests
polar	found in the high latitudes; cold, no trees and few flowering plants

Name _____ Date _____

© Pearson Education, Inc., publishing as Pearson Prentice Hall. All rights reserved.

Name _____ Date _____ Class _____

Latin America Study Sheet

Key Terms

aqueduct pipe or channel designed to carry water from a distant source

boom period of increased economic prosperity

campesino a poor farmer or a landless peasant

canopy dense mass of leaves that form the ceiling of a forest

Carnival a celebration held in Latin America each year just before Lent

caudillo military officer who ruled very strictly with unlimited powers

circumnavigate sail or fly all the way around something, such as the Earth

commonwealth a place that has its own government but also has strong ties to another country

conquistador conqueror; a Spanish soldier

constitution a statement of a country's basic laws

coral a rocklike substance formed from the accumulation of skeletons of tiny sea animals over hundreds of years

Creole a person born in the Caribbean of European, usually French, and African descent; a dialect spoken by Creoles

criollo a person with Spanish parents but who is born in Latin America; often wealthy and well-educated

dictator a ruler who has complete power

diversify to add variety

diversity variety

economy the ways that goods and services are produced and made available to people

ecotourism travel to unspoiled areas in order to observe wildlife and learn about the environment

El Niño a warming of the ocean water along the western coast of South America

elevation the height of land above sea level

emigrate to leave one country and settle in another

ethnic group a group of people who share the same ancestry, language, religion, or cultural traditions

export to send products from one country to be sold in another country; a product that is sold in another country

favela poor neighborhood in Brazil

gaucho cowhand; legendary nomadic cowboy

hacienda a plantation owned by Spaniards or the Catholic Church

hieroglyphics a system of writing using signs and symbols

hurricane a violent tropical storm, with high winds and torrential rain

hydroelectricity power produced by harnessing the energy of flowing water with huge dams

immigrant a person who has moved to one country from another

import to bring products into one country from another; a product brought from another country to sell

indigenous people who are descendants of the people who first lived in a region

injustice the unfair treatment of people

isthmus a narrow strip of land that has water on both sides and joins two larger bodies of land

ladino mestizo descended from Native Americans and Spaniards

land reform the effort to distribute the land more equally

Line of Demarcation an imaginary line from the North Pole to the South Pole at about 50°W longitude that gave Spain the right to settle and trade west of the line and Portugal the right to settle and trade east of the line

lock a section of waterway in which a ship is raised and lowered by adjusting the water level

maquiladora an American-owned factory, located in Mexico along the border of the United States

© Pearson Education, Inc., publishing as Pearson Prentice Hall. All rights reserved.

mestizo person of mixed Spanish and Native American descent

migrant worker worker who does not own land but who travels from one area to another, picking crops that are in season

one-resource economy economy in which only one resource or crop provides a majority of a country's income

pampas flat grassland region; the central plains in Argentina

plateau a large raised area of mostly level land

political movement a large group of people who work together for political change

privatization the government sale of its industries to individuals or private companies

refugee a person who leaves his homeland for personal safety or to escape persecution

regime a particular administration or government

revolution a political movement in which the people overthrow a government and set up another

rural having to do with countryside areas

sierra mountain region

squatter someone who settles on another's land without permission

strike refusal to work until certain demands of workers are met

subsistence farmer a rural person who grows only enough food for his or her family to eat

treaty an agreement in writing made between two or more countries

Treaty of Tordesillas signed by the Spanish and Portuguese in 1494 to establish the Line of Demarcation

tributary a river or stream that flows into a larger river

urban having to do with city areas

Key Places

Amazon rain forest a large area of abundant rainfall and dense vegetation in northern Brazil

Amazon River second-longest river in the world; flows from Peru into the Atlantic Ocean; contains about 20 percent of all the fresh water in the world

Amazon River Basin area consisting of plains, highlands, and Andes Mountains; contains the largest tropical rain forest in the world

Andes steep mountains along the western coast of South America that rise to heights of more than 20,000 feet (6,100 m) in some places

Argentina South American country with large, diverse cities and pampas, plains on which gauchos herd cattle

Atacama Desert barren land of little moisture on the coast of northern Chile

Brasília planned capital of Brazil; moved by the Brazilian government in an attempt to attract some people from the coastal areas to help develop industry using resources from the rain forest

Brazil South America's largest country; has been building up its various industries to diversify from its traditional standby, coffee; culturally diverse, its people speak Portuguese

Buenos Aires Argentine capital city; cosmopolitan and diverse, with a great variety of cultural activities

Canal Zone land on either side of the Panama Canal, including the ports, the port cities, and the railroad; governed by United States laws and control until 1999

Caracas Venezuelan capital city and center of government

Caribbean a region of small islands made up of coral and larger islands that are the tops of huge underwater mountains; also called the West Indies

Central America an isthmus of seven nations that connects Mexico with South America; dominated by coastal plains and steep, rugged mountains

Chile long, narrow South American country that has mountains, beaches, deserts, forests, and polar regions; most people in Chile are mestizos

Name _____ Date _____ Class _____

Copán Mayan religious center in present-day Honduras

Cuba largest Caribbean island; under a communist government

Cuzco village in the Andes settled by the Incas in about 1200 that became the center of the Incan Empire; now a city in the country of Peru

Guatemala Central American country with the largest population, the majority of which are Native American

Latin America located in the Western Hemisphere; includes all the nations from Mexico to the tip of South America and the Caribbean islands

Mexico area that stretches from the United States to Central America; dominated by mountains and a central plateau

Mexico City Mexico's capital and largest city, home to more than 23 million people; known for its dense air pollution and large differences between lifestyles of rich and poor

Nicaragua largest but least populated country in Central America; struggles with civil war and natural disasters

Panama Central American country through which the Panama Canal passes

Panama Canal water passage through Panama that connects the Pacific Ocean with the Atlantic Ocean

Patagonia cold, arid region of South America

Rio de Janeiro coastal Brazilian city; home to the rich and very poor

Santiago Chilean capital city that mixes Old Spanish buildings with new skyscrapers; troubled by pollution

South America continent that contains many types of landforms, including the Andes Mountains, the grasslands of the pampas, and the Amazon River Basin

Tenochtitlán Aztec center of trade and learning located on an island in Lake Texcoco; the site of present-day Mexico City

Trinidad and Tobago Caribbean islands that host the biggest Carnival

Valley of Mexico landform of Central Mexico that includes the site of present-day Mexico City; center of Aztec civilization

Venezuela a major oil-producing country of South America attempting to diversify its economy

Key People

Aristide, Jean-Bertrand democratically elected president of Haiti in 1990; forced out after seven months and returned in 1994; forced out again in 2004

Bolivár, Simón Latin American revolutionary leader who, by 1822, had freed a large area from Spanish rule: the future countries of Colombia, Venezuela, Ecuador, and Panama; eventually drove the remaining Spanish forces out of South America altogether

Columbus, Christopher Spanish-sponsored explorer who landed in the Caribbean Sea in 1492

Cortés, Hernán Spanish soldier who conquered the Aztecs in 1521

Hidalgo, Miguel criollo priest who encouraged revolution against the Spanish government; his call for revolution became known as the "Cry of Dolores"

Iturbide, Agustín de high-ranking officer in the Spanish army who led rebels to defeat the Spanish and declare Mexico independent in 1821

L'Ouverture, Toussaint former slave who led a revolt against French rule in Saint-Domingue (Haiti), the first colony in Latin America to start a revolution

Magellan, Ferdinand Portuguese explorer sailing for Spain whose expedition was the first to circumnavigate the globe

Moctezuma Aztec ruler who welcomed Cortés and then was killed by the Spanish

Pizarro, Francisco Spanish conquistador who had conquered most of the Incan Empire by 1535

San Martín, José de an Argentine who led soldiers to free Chile and Peru from Spanish rule

© Pearson Education, Inc., publishing as Pearson Prentice Hall. All rights reserved.

Name _____ Date _____ Class _____

Native American Groups of Latin America

Arawak South American group who lived on the Caribbean islands

Aztec arrived in the valley of Mexico in the 1100s; capital city was Tenochtitlán (present-day Mexico City)

Carib South American group who lived on the Caribbean islands; gave the region its name; only a few hundred reside on Dominica today

Ciboney native Americans who lived on the Caribbean islands for thousands of years

Inca lived in the Andes Mountains around 1200; excellent farmers, builders, and managers; empire stretched along Pacific Coast through Peru, Bolivia, Chile, and Argentina

Maya thrived in Central America and southern Mexico from about A.D. 300 to A.D. 900; left their cities but remained in region; still found in Mexico, Belize, Guatemala, Honduras, and El Salvador

Medieval Times to Today Study Sheet

Key Terms

absolute monarch a king or leader who has complete power over every part of life in a kingdom; for example, Louis XIV of France

Akbar the greatest Mughal leader of India

Allied Powers in World Wars I and II, the countries who formed an alliance to fight against Germany and its allies

Anasazi one of the ancient Native American peoples of the Southwest

apprentice an unpaid person training in a craft or trade

archipelago a group or chain of many islands

atomic bomb a powerful nuclear weapon developed and used during World War II

Axis Powers in World War II, the alliance of Germany, Italy, Japan, and other nations that opposed the Allied Powers

Aztecs a people who lived in the valley of Mexico

Bantu a large group of central and southern Africans who speak related languages

bushido a Japanese samurai warrior's set of rules that stressed honor, discipline, bravery, and simple living

caliph a Muslim ruler

caravan a group of traders traveling together for safety

census an official count of people in a certain place at a certain time

chivalry code of honorable conduct for knights

city-state a city that is also a separate independent state

clan a group of families who trace their roots to the same ancestor

clergy persons with authority to perform religious services

Cold War the tension between the United States and the Soviet Union from 1945-1991

colony a territory ruled by another nation, often one that is far away

communism a kind of government in which all people together own the farms and factories, share work equally, and earn rewards equally

conquistador a Spanish conqueror

Crusades a series of military expeditions launched by Christian Europeans to win the Holy Land back from Muslim control

czar the Russian emperor

divine right of kings the belief that the authority of kings comes directly from God

dynasty a series of rulers from the same family

Elizabethan Age the golden age of English history when Elizabeth I was queen

encomienda a system in which the Spanish king gave Spanish settlers the right to the labor of Native Americans who live in a particular area

Enlightenment philosophical movement, primarily of the 1700s, that was characterized by reliance on reason and experience

excommunication expelling someone from the Church

feudalism in Japan, a system in which poor people were legally bound to work for wealthy landowners; in the Middle Ages, a system in which land was owned by kings or lords but held by vassals in return for their loyalty

French Revolution a revolution in France that resulted in the overthrow of the French monarchy; it lasted from 1789 to 1799

genocide the systematic killing of an entire group of people

guild an association of all the people in a town or village who practiced a certain trade; for example, weavers, grocers, masons, and others in the Middle Ages who formed guilds and set standards for quality and prices

hajj for Muslims, a pilgrimage or sacred journey to Mecca

© Pearson Education, Inc., publishing as Pearson Prentice Hall. All rights reserved.

hieroglyphics the signs and symbols that made up the Mayan writing system

hijra the migration in A.D. 622 of Muslims from Mecca to Yathrib (now called Medina)

Hinduism a religion developed in India, introduced by the Aryans, and based on sacred books called the Vedas and Upanishads

Holocaust Nazi Germany's mass killing of Jewish people

humanism a system of thought that focuses on the nature, ideals, and achievements of human beings rather than on the divine

imperialism the effort of a nation to create an empire of colonies

Incas people of a powerful South American empire during the 1400s and 1500s

Industrial Revolution the change in methods of producing goods—from hand tools at home to machines in factories, 1760-1860

Islam the religion practiced by Muslims; based on the teaching of the prophet Muhammad and on the holy book of Islam, the Quran

Justinian's Code an organized collection and explanation of Roman laws for use by the Byzantine Empire

kiva a round room used by pueblo people for religious purposes

knight a man who received honor and land in exchange for serving a lord as a soldier

Kublai Khan a Mongol emperor of China

Magna Carta the "Great Charter"; in which the king's power over his nobles was limited; agreed to by King John of England in 1215

manor a large estate, often including farms and a village, ruled by a lord

Mayas a people who established a great civilization in Middle America

medieval referring to the Middle Ages

merit system a system of hiring people based on their abilities

Middle Ages the years between ancient and modern times

migration the movement from one country or region to another

millennium a period of one thousand years

mosque a Muslim house of worship

Mughal Empire a period of Muslim rule of India from the 1500s to the 1700s

Muhammad the prophet and founder of Islam

Muslim a follower of Islam

Napoleonic Code the French legal system based on Enlightenment ideals, set up during Napoleon's rule

nation a community of people that shares a territory and a government

nationalism a feeling of pride in one's country and a desire for its independence

natural rights rights that belong to all human beings from birth

Nazi Party a political party founded in Germany in 1919 and brought to power by Hitler in 1933

nomad people with no permanent home, who move from place to place in search of food, water, or pasture

oral history accounts of the past that people pass down by word of mouth

Parliament a council that advised the English king or queen in government matters

peasant a member of a class that makes its living through small-scale farming and labor

pilgrim a person who journeys to a sacred place

postwar after war; after World War II

prophet a religious leader or other person who claims to carry the message of God

Protestants referring to Christian religions that grew out of the Reformation

pueblo Native American stone or adobe buildings, part of a cluster of buildings

quipu a group of knotted strings used by the Incas to record information

Quran the holy book of Islam

Name _____ Date _____ Class _____

Reformation the effort to change or reform the Catholic Church which led to the establishment of Protestant churches

Reign of Terror the period of the French Revolution during which many people were executed for opposing the revolution

Renaissance the period of the rebirth of learning in Europe between about 1300 and 1600

revolution a complete overthrow of an established government; a sudden change in the way people think

Roman Catholicism a Christian religion that is headed by the Pope and has a hierarchical organization of cardinals, bishops, and priests

samurai Japanese warriors

Sanskrit an ancient language of India

savanna an area of grassland with scattered trees and bushes

schism a split, particularly in a church or religion

scientific method a method involving careful observation of nature and, in some sciences, controlled experiments

serf farm worker considered part of the manor on which he or she worked

shogun supreme military commander in Japan

slash-and-burn agriculture a type of farming in which trees are cut down and burned to clear and fertilize the land

Sufis Muslim group that believed they could draw closer to God through prayer, fasting, and a simple life

sultan a Muslim ruler

superpower a powerful country that can influence many other countries

Swahili a Bantu language with Arabic words, spoken along the East African coast

terrace a step like ledge cut into a mountainside, to make land suitable for farming

terrorism threat or use of violence to cause fear

textile industry cloth production

trading bloc a group of countries that has agreed to reduce barriers to trade

troubadour a traveling poet and musician of the Middle Ages

vassal a man who promised to be loyal to a landowner who, in return, gave him a share of the land (a fief)

Key Places

Place	Description
Aksum	an ancient town in northern Ethiopia
Andes	a mountain chain on the western coast of South America
Angkor Wat	the capital of an ancient Asian empire
Baghdad	the capital of the Muslim empire during Islam's golden age
Cahokia	a village in what is now the state of Illinois; formerly a large, prehistoric city known for its Native American mounds
Cairo	the capital and largest city of Egypt, located on the Nile River
Constantinople	the capital of the eastern Roman Empire and later of the Byzantine Empire
Cuzco	the capital city of the Incan Empire, located in present-day Peru
Florence	a city in the Tuscany region of central Italy
Gaul	a region of France, Belgium, and parts of Germany and northern Italy occupied by the ancient Gauls

© Pearson Education, Inc., publishing as Pearson Prentice Hall. All rights reserved.

Ghana	the first West African kingdom based on the gold and salt trade
Grand Canal	the 1,085-mile (1,747 km) channel connecting the Huang and Chang rivers in China; the longest artificially made waterway in the world
Great Plains	a mostly flat and grassy region of western North America
Great Zimbabwe	a powerful East African kingdom
Hiroshima	a city in the southwestern part of the island of Honshu, Japan; the first city to be hit by an atomic bomb dropped by the United States during World War II
Holy Land	Jerusalem and parts of the surrounding area where Jesus lived and taught
Incan Empire	an empire ruled by the Incas that stretched along the Andes
Jerusalem	a city in the Holy Land regarded as sacred by Christians, Muslims, and Jews
Kyoto	the capital city of medieval Japan
Lake Texcoco	the site of the ancient city of Tenochtitlán, capital of the Aztec empire
Machu Picchu	an ancient city in the Andes built during the Incan Empire
Mali	a rich kingdom of the West African savanna
Mecca	an Arabian trading center and Muhammad's birthplace
Medina	one of the two holiest city of Islam (the other being Mecca)
Nagasaki	a city on the island of Kyushu, Japan; the site of the second atomic bomb dropped by the United States during World War II
Pearl Harbor	an inlet of the Pacific Ocean on the southern coast of Hawaii
Red Sea	a narrow sea located between northeast Africa and the Arabian Peninsula; connected to the Mediterranean Sea in the north and the Arabian Sea in the south
Sahara	a huge desert stretching across most of North Africa
Silk Road	a chain of trade routes stretching from China to the Mediterranean Sea
Songhai	an ancient empire and trading state in West Africa
Strait of Magellan	waterway near the southern tip of South America
Versailles	palace built for the French king Louis XIV

The United States and Canada Study Sheet

Key Terms

abolitionist a person who believed that enslaving people was wrong and wanted to end the practice

agribusiness a large company that runs huge farms to produce, process, and distribute agricultural products

alliance a formal agreement to do business together, sometimes formed between governments

alluvial soil soils deposited by water; the fertile topsoil left by rivers after a flood

aquaculture the cultivation of fish and water plants

bilingual speaking two languages; having two official languages

boomtown a settlement that springs up quickly, often to serve the needs of miners

boycott a refusal to buy or use goods and services as a form of protest

capital money used to expand a business

civil rights movement a large group of people who worked together in the United States beginning in the 1960s to end the segregation of African Americans and support equal rights for all minorities

Civil War the war between the northern (the Union) and southern (the Confederacy) states in the United States, which began in 1861 and ended in 1865

Cold War a period of great tension between the United States and the former Soviet Union, which lasted for more than 40 years after World War II

Confederacy southern states that seceded from the United States and founded the Confederate States of America because of a fear that they would have little say in a government with a president from the North

Constitution, United States approved in 1789; established a government of three branches in which the government's powers are limited and individual citizens have rights that the government cannot take away

corporate farm a large farm run by a corporation; may consist of smaller farms once owned by families

cultural diversity a wide variety of cultures

cultural exchange a process in which different cultures share ideas and ways of doing things

Declaration of Independence statement issued in 1776 that explained why the American colonies were seeking independence from Britain; written by Thomas Jefferson

discrimination the practice of treating certain groups of people unfairly

dominion a self-governing area subject to ownership by another government

ethnic group a group of people who share the same ancestors, culture, language, or religion

exile to force to leave an area

export to send goods to another country for sale

forty-niner one of the first miners of the California Gold Rush of 1849

fossil fuel a source of energy formed over millions of years from animal and plant remains; products include coal, petroleum and natural gas

Francophone a person who speaks French as his or her first language

free trade a system of trade with no tariffs, or taxes, on imported goods

glacier a huge, slow-moving sheet of snow and ice

Homestead Act a law passed in 1862 giving 160 acres (65 hectares) of land on the Midwestern plains to any adult willing to live on and farm it for five years

hydroelectricity electric power generated by moving water

immigrant a person who moves to a new country in order to settle there

immunity a natural resistance to disease

import to bring goods into one country from another

Name _____ Date _____ Class _____

indentured servant a person who, in exchange for benefits received, must work for a period of years to gain freedom

indigenous belonging to and native of a certain place

industrialization the process of building new industries in an area dominated by farming; the development of large industries

Industrial Revolution the change from making goods by hand to making them by machine

Louisiana Purchase the sale of land in 1803 by France to the United States; all the land between the Mississippi River and the eastern slope of the Rocky Mountains

loyalist a colonist who was loyal to Great Britain during the American Revolution

Manifest Destiny a belief that the United States had a right to own all the land from the Atlantic Ocean to the Pacific Ocean

maritime related to navigation or commerce on the sea

mass transit a system of subways, buses, and commuter trains used to transport large numbers of people

megalopolis a number of cities and suburbs that blend into one very large urban area

melting pot a country in which all cultures blend together to form a single culture

mixed-crop farm a farm that grows several different kinds of crops

permafrost permanently frozen layer of ground below the top layer of soil

petrochemical a substance that is made from petroleum

population density the average number of people per square mile or square kilometer

prairie a region of flat or rolling land covered with tall grasses

province a political division of land in Canada, similar to a state in the United States

Quiet Revolution a peaceful change in the government of Quebec, Canada, in which the *Parti Québécois* won control of the legislature and made French the official language

quota only a certain number allowed

rain shadow an area on the sheltered side of a mountain, away from the wind, that receives little rainfall

recession a downturn in business activity and economic prosperity

Reconstruction United States plan for rebuilding the nation after the Civil War; including a period during which the South was governed by the Union Army

referendum a ballot or vote in which voters decide for or against a particular issue

reservation land set aside for a specific purpose, as by the United States government for Native Americans

Revolutionary War the war in which the American colonies won their independence from Britain; fought from 1775 to 1781

segregate to set apart and force to use separate schools, housing, parks, and so on because of race or religion

separatist in Canada, someone who wants the province of Quebec to break away from the rest of the country

terrorist a person who uses violence and fear to achieve political goals

transportation corridor a passageway through which people can travel by foot, vehicle, rail, ship, or airplane

treaty an agreement between two or more nations

tributary a river or stream that flows into a larger river

tropics the area on Earth between 23.5°N and 23.5°S lines of latitude, where the climate is almost always hot

tundra a cold, dry region covered with snow for more than half the year

Key Places

Appalachian Mountains a mountain system in eastern North America; meets with Laurentian Highlands in Canada

Canadian Shield region of ancient rock covered by a thin layer of soil; about half of Canada

© Pearson Education, Inc., publishing as Pearson Prentice Hall. All rights reserved.

Coast Mountains a mountain range in western Canada and southern Alaska

Continental Divide the boundary that separates rivers flowing to the Pacific Ocean from those flowing to the Atlantic Ocean

Death Valley the hottest, driest region of North America; located in southeastern California

Fraser River a major river of western North America, along the border between British Columbia and Alberta

Great Lakes a group of five lakes in central North America; Lakes Superior, Michigan, Huron, Erie, and Ontario

Jamestown first permanent British settlement in North America; founded in 1607 and located in present-day Virginia

Mississippi River a large river in the central United States flowing south from Minnesota to the Gulf of Mexico

Ottawa the national capital of Canada, located in Ontario

Pacific Rim the countries bordering the Pacific Ocean

Pennsylvania Colony a colony in America founded in 1682 by William Penn, who purchased land from the Native Americans

Rocky Mountains the major mountain range in western North America that extends south from Alberta, Canada, through the western United States down to Mexico

St. Lawrence Lowlands a major agricultural region in the prairie provinces of Canada

St. Lawrence River a river in eastern North America; the third-longest river in Canada

St Lawrence Seaway a navigable seaway from the Atlantic Ocean to the western end of the Great Lakes; maintained jointly by the United States and Canada

Sierra Nevada Mountains a mountain range in California in the western United States

Sun Belt a broad area of the United States, stretching from the southern Atlantic Coast to the coast of California

Washington, D.C. the national capital of the United States; located between the states of Maryland and Virginia on the Potomac River

Yukon a territory in northwestern Canada

Key People

Cartier, Jacques a French explorer who sailed up the St. Lawrence River near today's Quebec City

Jackson, Andrew elected president in 1828; supported the interest of poor farmers, laborers, and settlers who wanted Native American lands in the Southeast

King, Jr., Martin Luther leader of the civil rights movement to end segregation and win rights for African Americans

Lewis, Meriwether, and Clark, William sent by Thomas Jefferson in 1804 to explore land west of the Mississippi River

Lincoln, Abraham sixteenth president of the United States, 1861-1865; known for his effective leadership during the Civil War and the Emancipation Proclamation of 1863 that declared the end of slavery

Mackenzie, William leader against British rule in Upper Canada

Papineau, Louis a French Canadian who organized a revolt in Lower Canada to establish the region as a separate country

Riis, Jacob took readers on tours of tenement life in late 1800s in his book *How the Other Half Lives*

Roosevelt, Franklin D. took office as president in 1933; created New Deal plan to help people get jobs and to restore the economy

Truman, Harry S became president in April 1945 after the death of President Roosevelt

Growth of the United States

1783	The Treaty of Paris ended the American Revolution and Great Britain recognized the United States as an independent nation.
1803	President Thomas Jefferson bought the Louisiana Territory from France for $15 million, doubling the size of the United States.
1818	A treaty with Great Britain gave the United States the Red River Basin.
1819	The United States purchased Florida from Spain.
1842	After a long dispute between the United States and Great Britain, a treaty settled the Canadian border.
1845	The United States obtained the Republic of Texas after American settlers revolted against Mexican rule.
1846	The United States struck a deal with Great Britain to acquire the Oregon Country.
1848	The Treaty of Guadalupe Hidalgo, which officially ended the Mexican War, gave the United States over 535,000 square miles (1.4 million square kilometers) of land.
1853	The United States paid Mexico $10 million for land in the Gadsden Purchase.
1867	The United States purchased Alaska from Russia.
1898	The United States took control of Hawaii, Puerto Rico, Guam, and the Philippines.

The United States of America

State	Capital	State	Capital
Alabama	Montgomery	**Montana**	Helena
Alaska	Juneau	**Nebraska**	Lincoln
Arizona	Phoenix	**Nevada**	Carson City
Arkansas	Little Rock	**New Hampshire**	Concord
California	Sacramento	**New Jersey**	Trenton
Colorado	Denver	**New Mexico**	Santa Fe
Connecticut	Hartford	**New York**	Albany
Delaware	Dover	**North Carolina**	Raleigh
Florida	Tallahassee	**North Dakota**	Bismarck
Georgia	Atlanta	**Ohio**	Columbus
Hawaii	Honolulu	**Oklahoma**	Oklahoma City
Idaho	Boise	**Oregon**	Salem
Illinois	Springfield	**Pennsylvania**	Harrisburg
Indiana	Indianapolis	**Rhode Island**	Providence
Iowa	Des Moines	**South Carolina**	Columbia
Kansas	Topeka	**South Dakota**	Pierre

© Pearson Education, Inc., publishing as Pearson Prentice Hall. All rights reserved.

Name _____ Date _____ Class _____

State	Capital	State	Capital
Kentucky	Frankfort	**Tennessee**	Nashville
Louisiana	Baton Rouge	**Texas**	Austin
Maine	Augusta	**Utah**	Salt Lake City
Maryland	Annapolis	**Vermont**	Montpelier
Massachusetts	Boston	**Virginia**	Richmond
Michigan	Lansing	**Washington**	Olympia
Minnesota	St. Paul	**West Virginia**	Charleston
Mississippi	Jackson	**Wisconsin**	Madison
Missouri	Jefferson City	**Wyoming**	Cheyenne

Canadian Provinces

Province	Capital	Province	Capital
Alberta	Edmonton	**Nunavut**	Iqaluit
British Columbia	Victoria	**Ontario**	Toronto
Manitoba	Winnipeg	**Prince Edward Island**	Charlottetown
New Brunswick	Fredericton	**Quebec**	Quebec
Newfoundland and Labrador	St. John's	**Saskatchewan**	Regina
Northwest Territories	Yellowknife	**Yukon Territory**	Whitehorse
Nova Scotia	Halifax		

© Pearson Education, Inc., publishing as Pearson Prentice Hall. All rights reserved.